Tracing the exodus throughout Scripture

SLAVERY
TO
SERVANTHOOD

John H. White

GREAT COMMISSION PUBLICATIONS

7401 OLD YORK ROAD, PHILADELPHIA, PENNSYLVANIA 19126

led to this book by the Holy Spirit Rev. Rosalie Maxiel 12/24/2022

All scripture quotations are from the New International Version,
copyright © 1978 by International Bible Society.
Used by permission.

ISBN 0-934688-41-9

Printed in USA

Published by Great Commission Publications
7401 Old York Road, Philadelphia, Pennsylvania 19126

I Discoved this Dec, 24, 2025.

John H. "Jack" White

1936 - 2021

Memorial service at Geneva College / Rev. Dr. William Glaze — was one of the participants

1

WHY THE EXODUS THEME?

Frequently when you begin a new study you wonder if it will be worth your time. A study of the exodus does not raise this kind of doubt. Few events in history have so captured the attention of God's people; young and old alike find something to interest them in this historic event. And there are other benefits as well, for an understanding of the exodus is a key to applying and appreciating the message of both the Old and New Testaments.

The word *exodus* means "departure," a theme that occupies a central place in the history of God's dealing with his people. As you study this theme you will confront a number of different issues. You will see God's mighty acts described in vivid detail and his grace lovingly portrayed.

The entire Bible reflects on the events recorded in the book of Exodus, which shows how God made provisional deliverance for Israel. Both Old and New Testaments abound with allusions to what the exodus meant to Israel and what it means to all the people of God. As you master the exodus theme its message will bless and challenge you in your own life as a Christian.

Your understanding of the redemptive work of Christ will be enhanced as you see this Old Testament theme repeated throughout the New. You will discover that it was not by coincidence that Moses and Elijah spoke with Jesus about his departure or exodus (Luke 9:31). We are meant to see that their earthly ministries were connected. In the desert Moses sang his song in response to God's saving work. Someday all of us who belong to Christ will sing the song of Moses and the Lamb in the new heavens and the new earth. If that song will one day be ours we should know something of the biblical background of the words we will sing.

Our study of the exodus begins with the Old Testament book of that name. The name of the book is not derived from a Hebrew title but from a third-century-BC Greek translation called the Septuagint. Almost all the marvelous narrative of the book relates to the events surrounding the going-out of God's people from Egypt.

The story begins with Israel as an enslaved people. God hears their cries and raises up a deliverer. Then comes the violent clash between the true God of Israel and the false gods of Egypt. Plague after plague descends on the stubborn, unbelieving Pharaoh and the nation he rules, culminating in the last horrible plague of death. Egypt suffers, but the angel of death passes over Israel and they are set free.

But this is not the entire story, for the great purpose of God had been to set his people free *to serve him*. We are shocked by the rebellion of the Israelites in the wilderness and overwhelmed by God's grace in the covenant made at Sinai. The exodus from the old ways of living proved much more difficult than the exodus from the old land of bondage. In subsequent chapters God slowly and lovingly reveals the symbolic meaning of the atonement and his fellowship with his people in the tabernacle.

How can such an ancient event be relevant today? We live in the twentieth century and experience its culture; how can such a biblical theme apply to us? Many forces of bondage are evident in our culture. Ironically, while technology advances and culture and science develop, our drive to be free is frustrated by a growing lack of personal satisfaction, rising economic insecurity, racial tension, international terrorism, and value confusion in a pluralistic society. All of these phenomena bring their own enslavement.

This problem is not something that concerns only scholars or artists. None of us needs to look very far to see the devastating reality of the enslavement resulting from drug or alcohol abuse, the breakup of marriage and the home, the materialistic and hedonistic life-styles so typical of our age. Men and women are in bondage because they rely on temporal substitutes for God such as national privilege, tradition, religious ceremonies, slavish adherence to law, and love of self.

This enslavement is more than just personal: entire societies and governments, not unlike Egypt, are oppressing the poor and hungry. More significantly, they oppress the people of God as they attempt to serve the Lord in the education of their children and their public witness for Christ. These governments are guilty of religious, racial and economic oppression and refuse to protect human life and provide freedom for the full expression of faith.

One day while writing this book I decided to sample an evening's television fare. I saw being advertised products and experiences beyond a king's reach. Commercials included automatic garage-door openers, designer jeans to make you sexy, perfumes guaranteed to make you a good lover, a special one-way trip to Florida that "anyone can afford."

What was happening that night was spiritual formation far more effective than any totalitarian bondage. I was experiencing the constant electronic suasion that whets our appetites for more while closing our eyes and hardening our hearts to the consequences of materialism in our own lives and in a needy world. Even some of the television preachers tell us that prosperity is evidence of God's blessing and, by implication, that poverty is a sign of God's disfavor.

The Roots of Bondage

These and many other modern forms of bondage are rooted in our alienation from God, and Genesis 3 describes these roots. Our physical and spiritual parents, Adam and Eve, were called to live in the freedom of friendship with and obedience to God. But they forsook that freedom in favor of the supposed freedom of their own way and the attractions of the devil. Rather than submitting to God's sovereignty they went their own way and rejected the goodness of God. Men and women became autonomous —free from God but slaves to self.

Genesis 3:7-24 describes sin's oppression and bondage, the shame and guilt of Adam's and Eve's nakedness and their pathetic attempts to cover their guilt. The fig leaves of verse seven symbolize all human attempts to deal with guilt. The way Adam and Eve blamed each other for their guilt sounds so very contemporary. The ever-widening impact of the curse leads to cultural, familial and social bondage. The curse because of sin causes toil and frustration (read *enslavement*) in everything from childbearing to work.

The Bible dramatically reminds us that the ultimate oppression is death itself. It is the ultimate sentence upon all who rebel against God (Gen. 2:17; 3:19). This death is physical, spiritual, and potentially eternal. It is physical because sin brings death to our lives; if Adam and Eve had obeyed God, apparently they would have lived forever physically. But most significantly, death means spiritual separation from God. "[Y]ou were dead in your transgressions and sins" (Eph. 2:1; see Ps. 66). Ultimately it can mean everlasting separation from God in what the Bible calls "hell." Death hangs like a Sword of Damocles over our heads. We are its slave, desperately needing liberation.

The marvelous message of the exodus theme is that there is hope. Jesus conquered the cause of our bondage, and our death sentence is commuted through the exodus (departure) of Jesus in his sin-atoning death at Jerusalem. We will study more of that later, but suffice it now to say that the exodus provides the great biblical theme for a world in bondage and hopelessness. " 'Death has been swallowed up in victory.' 'Where, O death, is your victory? Where, O death, is your sting?' . . . But thanks be to God! He gives us the victory through our Lord Jesus Christ" (1 Cor. 15:54, 55, 57).

The Exodus Points to Christ

We must see the meaning of the exodus in the light of the work of Jesus Christ. Sometimes people perceive the exodus story as a series of moral and spiritual lessons for the people of God. For example, Moses is held up as a model believer in the midst of a sinful culture. We are told that, just as Moses was an example of faithfulness in the midst of Egyptian culture, so we must regard loyalty to the people of God as more important than any allegiance to this world.

There is some validity to this approach, but our study will show a different way of studying and understanding Scripture. The Bible is primarily the history of redemption. When the pattern of promise and fulfillment is ignored we miss much of what Scripture was intended to teach us. When we study the Old Testament we must be looking for the many ways it anticipates the New. This is so because from Genesis to Revelation Christ is the center of the biblical story. Any proper study must always look ahead to the one who is greater than Moses and to the ultimate Passover offered to us through him. When we study Scripture in this way we still learn lessons of obedience and example. But we understand in a deeper way that they are grounded in a saving relationship to Christ.

The Background to Our Story

This principle also reminds us that many portions of Scripture look back to previous promises. Exodus cannot be understood without Genesis. We will discuss later the fulfillment of a threefold promise made to Abraham. In Genesis 12-15 God promises to make the descendants of

Abram a nation and a source of blessing to the world, as well as giving them a land. The rest of the Pentateuch tells how God acts in history to fulfill these promises.

In the exodus Israel became a *nation*, in contrast to a clan of nomads or a group of slaves. As a climax to the wilderness wanderings they entered the *land* of promise (the book of Joshua describes these events). By means of the law given at Sinai for their worship and for the governing of their personal and corporate lives, they were set apart to be a holy nation and thus prepared to be a *blessing* to the nations. Even the historical setting of the early chapters of Exodus is the fulfillment of another word from God to Abraham: "Then the LORD said to him, 'Know for certain that your descendants will be strangers in a country not their own, and they will be enslaved and mistreated four hundred years. But I will punish the nation they serve as slaves, and afterward they will come out with great possessions' " (Gen. 15:13, 14).

It is therefore important that we briefly review Genesis 46-48, where we see God overruling the perverted plans of Joseph's brothers and making Joseph Pharaoh's chief ruler instead. When famine came to the land of Canaan Joseph's position made it possible for the house of Jacob to survive on the provisions of Egypt. We see the dramatic reunion of Joseph with his brothers and watch Jacob move his family of seventy to the safety of Egypt. Pharaoh received Jacob with great honor and gave him the land of Goshen as his home.

But later the honored status of Israel gave way to slavery. "Then a new king, who did not know about Joseph, came to power in Egypt" (Ex. 1:8). Egypt was conquered by a Semitic people known as "Hyksos," or "shepherd kings." These foreign people composed dynasties fourteen through seventeen of Egyptian history. In the seventeenth dynasty the native Egyptians threw off this foreign rule. It is likely that the Egyptian revolt which ended the Hyksos rule resulted in a new pharaoh who forgot about Joseph and remembered only that the Israelites were like the hated Hyksos. The new pharaoh was determined to reduce them to a state where they could never aid a foreign invader.

Try to envision the starkness and cruelty of this slavery. It was more than abstract political oppression. The Egyptians were in the process of erecting stone obelisks weighing thousands of tons. Many of their temples and other buildings are still standing. The "machinery" that built these huge structures consisted of thousands of foreign slaves, among whom were the Israelites.

Some have suggested that the book of Exodus was used by the early church as a manual for people living as believers in an alien culture. We in our own cultural situation could benefit from a study of the exodus in its full biblical context.

Review Questions

1. What does *exodus* mean?

2. What is the root of our bondage?

3. What is the ultimate oppressor?

Discussion Questions

1. How do some governments enslave God's people?

2. Explain this statement: "Christ is the center of the biblical story." How does that affect the way we read the Old Testament? the way we understand the exodus?

2

EXODUS — AN ABRAHAM CONNECTION

Two thousand years before Christ Egypt was the most powerful nation in the world. At that time the strongest king that Egypt ever had was ruling the nation. Thutmose III was renowned throughout the world as a military conqueror and a great statesman. His wife Hatshepsut was as remarkable as her husband. She sent great trading expeditions to central Africa to gather goods and wealth in order to build great temples. Here was a powerful man and an extravagant wife, glamorous figures in what could be an intriguing narrative.

But the central figures in one of the greatest events of biblical history are not this powerful and prestigious couple but a group of slaves living in the area of Goshen — the Israelites. We focus on this downtrodden group not for their superior qualities but because of their role as central figures in God's great plan to save human beings from sin and death. In the history of redemption these lowly Israelites occupy center stage from the beginning. They illustrate what the biblical message always stresses — that our striving for obedience is itself an outgrowth of God's grace and love. God loved his people, and thus they became his.

The Promise to Abraham

From the very beginning God promised to send a savior into the world. When sin entered the world God promised that he would provide a child, born of a woman, who would deal a deathblow to Satan (Gen. 3:15). This promised seed was preserved in Noah and continued through Abraham. We learn much more about the way God will keep his promise of a savior from his calling of Abraham to follow him. God promised Abraham that he would make his descendants a great nation, give them a land, and bless all the world through them. Genesis 17:6-8 contains a specific promise to Abraham that his descendants would someday be a large and powerful nation. This promise was a far cry from Abraham's situation at the time — his marriage to Sarai had not produced even one child! God's promise, "I will make nations of you, and kings will come from you" (Gen. 17:6), seemed like a rhapsodic, impossible dream. But Abraham believed God and received these promises by faith, though he lived to see only the smallest beginnings of their fulfillment. Isaac, the son later provided by God, literally carried within him the seed of the redeemer who would be the promise's ultimate fulfillment. The drama on Mount Moriah, when God provided a ram instead of taking Isaac as a sacrifice, is another reminder of God's provision.

God later renewed these promises to Isaac and Jacob. He changed Jacob's name to Israel, whose sons became the fathers of the twelve tribes of Israel. The sons of Israel moved to Egypt 450 years before the exodus, driven there by great famine. God had insured the preservation of his people by making one of Israel's sons, Joseph, second only to Pharaoh in the land of Egypt at that crucial moment.

During the many years in Egypt Israel grew to be a great nation. When they entered Egypt "The descendants of Jacob numbered seventy in all . . . . but the Israelites were fruitful and multiplied greatly and became exceedingly numerous, so that the land was filled with them" (Ex. 1:5, 7). This biblical hyperbole used by Moses undoubtedly reminded his audience of what God had promised to Abraham. The Israelites were not yet organized into a nation, nor were they in their own land; but God would keep his promises and show his saving power. The exodus story records that step in his redemptive plan.

Our God always keeps his promises. Knowing this, we can wait in confident faith for him to act. The events preceding the exodus are a contest between Yahweh, Israel's God, and the gods of Egypt. The complex Egyptian religion defies schematization, but it appears that either man or the elements of creation were deified. Worship of the sun and the Nile River are two examples of the latter. Egyptian religion had no personal side to it, concerning itself rather with magical formulas and mummification. This typifies one of the essential differences between biblical religion and pagan religions, especially nature religions. Pagan gods are the same forever. There is no action, no history, no progress, no fulfillment, no end to history —just a continuing, inevitable cycle of nature. In contrast the God and Father of Jesus Christ makes promises—and acts in history to keep them.

The biblical pattern of promise and fulfillment strikes us as most relevant at this moment, one of the darkest in human history. In the midst of the seeming hopelessness bred by Egyptian oppression, God acted to keep his promise. In the history of the church as well as in the history of redemption, God brings renewal and reformation to his people when all hope seems lost, often with a measure of cultural and corporate victory as well.

Jesus reminds us that, even in the blackest days of human existence, all the rebellions and political and social upheaval are merely "the beginning of birth pains" (Matt. 24:8) for a new age. As the great promise-keeper, he reminds us that all evil and suffering will lead to the consummation of the Kingdom at his second coming. Most Bible expositors suggest that the event described in the early part of Matthew 24 refers, at least to some extent, to the ugly battles between the Jews and the Romans which came to a climax in the destruction of Jerusalem in AD 70. However, Matthew also uses the future tense to say that there will be wars and rumors of wars, famine and earthquakes. Surely Jesus had in view all of the ugly, traumatic events of wars and political and social upheaval throughout history. Yet God will act to keep his promise: " 'Yes, I am coming soon.' Amen. Come, Lord Jesus" (Rev. 22:20).

God Remembers His Promise

The exodus and the events surrounding it are rooted in the promises made to Abraham, Isaac and Jacob, as the Scriptures themselves explicitly declare. Under the oppressive burden of slavery the Israelites cried out and God heard their cry. He "remembered his covenant with Abraham, with Isaac and with Jacob. So God looked on the Israelites and was concerned about them" (Ex. 2:24, 25). When the Bible says that God remembers, it does not mean that he had earlier forgotten something: it is a way of expressing in human terms the faithfulness of God. This is in utter contrast to the pagan gods, who reflect all the whims and tantrums of their human creators. This principle is the foundation of hope for God's people in times of despair. Soon God will call upon Israel to remember what he has done in his mighty deliverance. But more of that later, when we look specifically at the Passover.

God's promises to Abraham and his offspring are mentioned again in Exodus 3:6. When God first calls Moses to be his instrument of deliverance he identifies himself by saying, "I am the God of your father, the God of Abraham, the God of Isaac and the God of Jacob." The Lord goes on to tell Moses that the Israelites would recognize the authenticity of this call when Moses told them, "The LORD, the God of your fathers, the God of Abraham, the God of Isaac and the God of Jacob, has sent me to you" (Ex. 3:15). God identifies himself as the God of promise. He is going to do something new and shattering, yet it is simply the way the God of the covenant keeps his promise. Even the miracles, the credentials of Moses' authority, were given "so that they may believe that the LORD, the God of their fathers—the God of Abraham, the God of Isaac and the God of Jacob—has appeared to you" (Ex. 4:5). Moses will be told a new name for God: "I AM WHO I AM." This name is a new revelation to the people of God and reveals something about his promise-keeping. Among other things this new name reveals God's nature as a totally independent, self-contained being who will keep whatever promises he makes, one who is not limited by any earthly circumstance (see Ex. 6:3). God heard the groaning of his people and prepared to judge Pharaoh and free them. He instructed Moses to say to the Israelites, "I am the LORD, and I will bring you out from under the yoke of the Egyptians . . . . And I will bring you to the land I swore with uplifted hand to give to Abraham, to Isaac and to Jacob. I will give it to you as a possession. I am the LORD" (Ex. 6:6, 8). At every major turn in the events of the exodus God reminds us of the Abraham connection.

In their personal and corporate lives God's people often find themselves in seemingly hopeless situations. We can be overwhelmed, both personally and corporately, by the opposition of a world dominated by the oppressive forces of secularism. But our great hope is in this, that our God is the God of Abraham, Moses, Paul, Timothy, *et al.* What he has spoken in his word he will do in history; we can be confident, then, "that he who began a good work in you will carry it on to completion until the day of Christ Jesus" (Phil. 1:6). This great covenant promise is for the people of God in every age.

> Great and marvelous are your deeds, Lord God
> Almighty.
> Just and true are your ways, King of the ages.
> Who will not fear you, O Lord, and bring glory to
> your name?
> For you alone are holy.
> All nations will come and worship before you, for
> your righteous acts have been revealed (Rev. 15:3, 4).

> He who testifies to these things says, "Yes, I am coming soon." Amen. Come, Lord Jesus (Rev. 22:20).

The Sign of the Covenant

This passage records a puzzling incident that took place before the exodus. Moses and his family were returning to Egypt following a long sojourn in the land of Midian. They spent a night at a lodging-place, where a strange thing happened: "[T]he LORD met Moses and was about to kill him" (Ex. 4:24). Then his wife Zipporah circumcised their son with a knife, and touched the knife to Moses' feet.

The Abraham connection enables us to understand this unusual occurrence. When God instituted his covenant with Abraham, he established that a man who entered the covenant by personal confession was required to bind himself and his family to covenant faithfulness by circumcising himself and his sons. The penalty for failure to meet this requirement was separation from the covenant. Moses had failed so to consecrate his son and thus was in peril of the judgment. The verses before and after Exodus 4:24-26 speak of Moses' commission to demand that Pharaoh let God's covenant people go to serve the Lord. But how could Moses dare to lead the people of God when he had neglected to consecrate his own son?

Circumcision symbolized putting away all that is displeasing to God and dedicating oneself to the task ahead. Outwardly it signified both cleansing and dedication. Inwardly the covenant it represented demanded of Abraham and his descendants a consecration to God — consecration that involved a response to God's prior grace and calling (Gen. 17:10).

Today much of our thinking about our faith is individualistic: we speak of a personal faith and personal commitments. But the Bible reminds us that God deals with families; because of that, the sign of entrance into the covenant relationship (circumcision) was to be administered not just to the father but also to his male children.

In the New Testament the sign of circumcision is replaced by the sacrament of Baptism. Both are meant to serve as solemn reminders of God's promises. Whether we receive the sign of the covenant as children or as adults, we must embrace the God to whom we are consecrated if we hope to receive his promises. The reverse is also true: if we fail to embrace the God of the covenant after receiving the sign of the covenant (circumcision then, baptism now) it becomes a sign of judgment. If we fail to embrace the God of the covenant we are cut off from the promises of the covenant. Moses' frightening encounter with God in Exodus 4:24 dramatizes the need for regular consecration to God. Without regular, deliberate decisions to give ourselves to the Lord we will drift away from him. The sacraments of Baptism and the Lord's Supper offer us worship opportunities to surrender afresh to Christ.

The introduction of circumcision intrudes into the exodus story and opens our eyes to the fact that Israel, God's firstborn, and God's servant Moses deserve to be cut off — to die because of their sin. Only Zipporah's blood-smearing rite averts Moses' death, a fact that takes on deeper meaning when we come to the blood of the lamb in the Passover ritual. The Passover follows the Lord's command that Moses tell Pharaoh, "Let my son go, so he may worship me." But Pharaoh refused to let him go; so God promised to kill his firstborn son (Ex. 4:23). This vignette in the flow of biblical history reminds us that the themes of sin, judgment, and redemption through atonement are the central messages of Scripture. All the promises of God find their focus in God's great redemptive work in Christ. "For no matter how many promises God has made, they are 'Yes' in Christ. And so through him the 'Amen' is spoken by us to the glory of God" (2 Cor. 1:20).

Perhaps as you read this you are facing a dark hour in your personal life or in that of your church. Perhaps you have shed many tears over a rebellious child. The Dutch

Christian, Corrie Ten Boom, sheltered Jews from Nazi death camps as an expression of her commitment to Christ. Eventually she and her sister were captured and taken to the infamous Nazi women's prison, Ravensbrück. By the intervention of God the Nazis allowed her to keep her Bible. Corrie led Bible studies in Barracks 28 inside that ugly and frightening women's concentration camp. Many prisoners lost the will to live and died in despair, but the promises read from Scripture so influenced the women of Barracks 28 that it became known as a place of hope. The word of promise from the sovereign, promise-keeping God brings hope in the darkest situations.

Whether we face bondage in Egypt, the concentration camps of Nazi Germany or the fears of our own lives, as believers we have hope. Have faith in God! What he has promised to perform, he will do.

> Praise be to the God and Father of our Lord Jesus Christ! In his great mercy he has given us new birth into a living hope through the resurrection of Jesus Christ from the dead, and into an inheritance that can never perish, spoil or fade — kept in heaven for you (1 Pet. 1:3, 4).

Review Questions

1. What was God's promise to Abraham? What was Abraham's response?

2. What does it mean to say that God remembers?

3. What did God reveal about himself in his call to Moses?

Discussion Questions

1. Cite examples in church history where God has brought renewal and reformation to his people. How do these examples follow the promise-and-fulfillment pattern?

2. How has God fulfilled his promise in your family? in your church?

3

BONDAGE AND HOPE

Our study of the Abraham connection reminds us of the great biblical pattern of promise and fulfillment. God promised Abraham that he would give him a land and make his children a great nation that would be a blessing to the world. The opening chapters of Exodus show us a major step in the fulfillment of the promises. Israel will become a body of God's people rather than just a group of nomads. Also, the powerful hope of life in the promised land, once seemingly lost in the testing of Egyptian bondage, revives to become powerful and relevant. God keeps his promises and that alone brings hope.

Israel: From Family to Nation

Because of the promise-and-fulfillment pattern, we should not think of Exodus as an entirely new book, for it continues the book of Genesis. The opening words, "These are the names of the sons of Israel," underline the link to the history of the patriarchs. But it is also a new step: this is the last time that the term *sons of Israel* refers to Jacob's immediate family. The phrase has been determined by Genesis 35:10—"[Y]ou will no longer be called Jacob; your name will be Israel." As God fulfills his promise by this step in the history of redemption, he no longer uses the title to refer to a nomadic family; henceforth it will be used in Scripture to refer to God's nation. From now on, in the history of revelation, the phrase *sons of Israel* will identify the whole people of God.

Sons of Israel/ *Sons of Jacob*	*Sons of Israel/* *Nation of God's People*
Genesis 35:10 ⟷ Exodus 1:1	Exodus 1:9 and following

Thus the history of redemption has taken a major step forward. It has moved from the family history of the patriarchs to a nation group known as the Lord's people. The transition is recorded by the simple statement that the sons of Jacob died (Ex. 1:6) and a period of time elapsed during which the descendants of Jacob multiplied and became a *people* living in Egypt.

A look at the roots of the hope of Jacob and Joseph for an exodus should be an encouragement to us. The sons of Jacob had sold their brother Joseph as a slave into Egypt. Genesis reminds us that Joseph has been lifted from slavery and imprisonment to near-supreme authority and power in the Egyptian government. God accomplished his purposes by using the cruel sin of Joseph's brothers to establish ultimately Joseph's exalted position. Genesis 47:13-31 describes the famine that came on the whole Near East and the way God provided for the sons of Jacob in Egypt.

Sandwiched into the narrative is the story (Gen. 47:29-31) of Jacob's impending death and the promise he elicits from Joseph that he will not be buried in Egypt. Jacob believed that the sojourn in Egypt was but an interlude in the great promises of God and that ultimately the sons of

Israel would possess the land God had promised. He required from Joseph an oath that he would be faithful to his promise. When Jacob was ready to die he gave specific instructions that he be buried with Abraham, Isaac and Sarah in the cave of Machpelah. Jacob and his people did not belong in the Egypt of Joseph but in the land promised to Abraham and his seed. Genesis 50:1-5 describes Joseph's faithfulness to his pledge to bury his father in Canaan. In Genesis 50:25 Joseph makes a similar request concerning his own burial: "God will surely come to your aid, and then you must carry my bones up from this place."

This Old Testament hope of life in a promised land is very powerful. It is especially forceful when it comes near the end of a book where humankind has traveled from Eden to a coffin, the chosen people from Canaan to Egypt. In contrast to the sentence of death in Genesis 2:17, "[Y]ou will surely die," the burial of Jacob and Joseph in the land of promise symbolizes a hope beyond the grave, a hope for restoration to Eden and fellowship with God. In concrete terms, the land and a burial place signified the promise. "The whole land of Canaan . . . I will give as an everlasting possession to you and your descendants after you; and I will be their God" (Gen. 17:8). But it was more than just real estate or a graveyard: "All these people were still living by faith when they died. They did not receive the things promised; they only saw them and welcomed them from a distance. . . . [T]hey were longing for a better country — a heavenly one" (Heb. 11:13, 16). Jacob and Joseph reached out for the promise even in the face of death. For Joseph there was no funeral procession like Jacob's. The fulfillment would await the timing of God and a better exodus. Joseph's words epitomize the hope of the Old Testament believer. Our faith falls into the same kind of expectant silence. "He who testifies to these things says, 'Yes, I am coming soon' " (Rev. 22:20). Joseph's words of faith and hope were, "God will surely come to your aid" (Gen. 50:24).

Expectant hope provides an essential element for life in general and the Christian life in particular. Victor Frankl, a Jewish psychiatrist who spent extended time in a Nazi prison camp during World War II, discovered that the only thing that guarded against barbarism and dehumanization in the concentration camp was some form of hope. Without it the prisoners more often than not would curl into a fetal position and die. But when there was some reason for hope — for release or a letter or some kind of better future—men and women lived beyond all odds. A Christian needs hope. Faith is being sure of what we hope for (Heb. 11:1). Such hope powerfully sustains believers since its foundation rests not on a wish but on a certainty based on God's word of promise. Believers look for the blessed hope of heaven, a new heaven and a new earth.

But what is faith? Surely it cannot be the romanticizing of our trials and burdens. The exodus period is a stark reminder that the focus of faith is not the subjective *strength* of our faith. It is not as though our faith had some kind of power or efficiency in itself. The most important thing is the *object* of our faith, the living God who keeps his promise. Because Israel knew God both experientially and theologically they believed that he would act to bring the sons of Israel out of Egypt. Surely the God who provided for barren Sarah and sustained Israel in time of famine could deliver his people out of Egypt. More than that, he had promised he *would* deliver Israel! "Blessed is he whose help is the God of Jacob" (Ps. 146:5).

Israel in Bondage

How did the children of Israel fare in the land of Egypt? At first they were well-received. Foreigners in the land, especially Asian immigrants, had often been welcomed into Egypt. The comparative freedom and peace described in the biblical record fits well with what we can discern from non-biblical records. But after Joseph's brothers and that generation had passed away, Israel increased and grew numerous and strong (Ex. 1:6, 7). Then the situation changed radically. This is expressed in Exodus 1:8—"Then a new king, who did not know about Joseph, came to power in Egypt." Then began a different life for Israel. It would seem likely that this refers to the expulsion of the Hyksos dynasty, who were of foreign blood, by new kings in the eighteenth dynasty, who were of pure Egyptian blood. Suddenly everything had changed: the Israelites were suspects instead of privileged guests.

Who are these new kings, and how long has it been since Joseph's death? Moses had not forgotten the details, but the real purpose of the narrative is to remind us that God acts in the exodus. Names, titles and statistics play only an insignificant role in a story that focuses on Israel's hope—the victorious act of God.

How did Israel fare in the house of bondage? The first six chapters of Exodus describe what their life was like. Exodus 6:9 summarizes their situation as "discouragement and cruel bondage." Evidently it was the rise of the new king in the nineteenth dynasty that is described in the biblical record. Extra-biblical sources enable us to understand something of the change that came about as the new king ascended the throne. Rameses II speaks of using foreigners "to haul stones for the god Re." Diodorus, an obscure recorder of that time, reports concerning the building of Rameses: "The most difficult of all these works were executed by the captives whom he had brought from foreign regions and he took care that the lapidary inscriptions should remind the reader that 'no Egyptian had a hand in them.' "[1]

Picture in your mind the harshness of this forced labor. The vivid description in Exodus 1:14 comes alive with the pathos of their enslavement: "They [the Egyptians] made their lives bitter with hard labor in brick and mortar and with all kinds of work in the fields; in all their hard labor the Egyptians used them ruthlessly." This enslavement broke the Israelites physically. The lash of the taskmaster, the scanty food supply, the impossible quotas, the heat of the blazing sun — all took their toll. They were broken psychologically also, because a power that enslaves the body enslaves the mind and spirit as well.

Mental enslavement dehumanizes and discourages even more than does physical harshness. The slavery of the American black did include physical abuse, but more dehumanizing to their lives has been its effect on the mind. To this day blacks struggle to believe that they really belong to American society. Their self-appreciation is still attacked by the mindset of enslavement.

Beyond the hardships imposed on the Israelites, they would not have been able to worship and serve the Lord with energy and devotion. For many of us a twelve-hour day of labor and the mentally draining demands of our jobs make it almost impossible to serve the Lord. The result can often be too little time for family or for full participation in the life of the church. So much of modern materialism and hedonism rob us of a full and hearty service of the Lord. Because of the subtle but powerful effect of enslavement on their minds and self-understanding, the Israelites were unable to say with any form of hearty affirmation, "We are the people of God."

Not only did the oppression remove the danger of an Israelite revolt, but Pharaoh hoped that by the sheer exhaustion of their slavery he could reduce their birthrate. "But the more they were oppressed, the more they multiplied and spread" (Ex. 1:12).

So the king of Egypt developed a more radical plan: he would weaken Israel by the systematic extermination of their newborn sons. Pharaoh summoned two Egyptian midwives and ordered them to kill the newborn Hebrew male children. In Egypt it was customary for mothers to crouch down on a pair of bricks or stones for birth. Egyptian histories record how a midwife would take a child in her arms, cut the umbilical cord, wash the baby, put it on a brick bench, and then announce the birth to the father. This practice seems to be alluded to in the "delivery stool" of Exodus 1:16.

The midwives refused to obey Pharaoh, not out of compassion for the babies or a desire to frustrate Pharaoh, but because they feared God. They knew something about the God of the Israelites. Their intimate association with the Israelites at the joyous and precious moment of birth enabled them to see and hear many expressions of the grace and promise of the Lord in the lives of the Israelites. We can imagine Israelite mothers and fathers singing or shouting praises to the Lord for his provision. The God of Abraham was keeping his promise! So the midwives feared the invisible God of the Israelites more than the visible power of the king.

Pharaoh asked, "Why have you done this? Why have you let the boys live?" The midwives answered Pharaoh, "Hebrew women are not like Egyptian women; they are vigorous and give birth before the midwives arrive" (Ex. 1:18, 19). Apparently they took the command from Pharaoh quite literally, believing that they were required to kill boy babies only at the moment of birth. Is it possible that they delayed their arrival until the birth was complete? We do not know whether the midwives were lying or whether it was a biological fact that Israelite women had quick births. If the midwives' answer was a "white lie," it was not their deceitfulness that was commended but their refusal to take a life. It has even been suggested that the Egyptian midwives used a word that is sometimes translated "vigorous" when referring to livestock. So they might have been using a derogatory term in reference to Israelite women, thus escaping Pharaoh's wrath.

Though this narrative of Scripture stresses God's protection for Israel, it contains a parenthetical message about the preciousness of human life. The Egyptian midwives feared God, but we are not told that they embraced God or entered into the circle of the covenant community. Yet even in this pagan nation those close to the beauty and marvel of human birth had respect for life. The horror of abortion in our modern culture must be continually opposed. If a pagan culture could recognize the sanctity of human life, how much more ought Christians? One way of dynamic witness will be our own rejoicing over and caring for our newborn. "Sons are a heritage from the

LORD, children a reward from him. . . . He settles the barren woman in her home as a happy mother of children. Praise the LORD" (Pss. 127:3; 113:9).

Thus far we have seen four measures used to enslave and oppress Israel. Each measure prompted God's countermeasure:

Pharaoh's Act	*God's Countermove*
1. Forced labor (Ex. 1:11)	1. Increase and growth of Israel (Ex. 1:12)
2. Increase and growth of Israel 2. Forced labor and cruelty (1:14)	2. Increase and growth of Israel (1:15-18)
3. Order to kill male babies (1:15, 16)	3. Increase and growth of Israel (1:20)
4. Order to throw male babies into the Nile (1:22)	4. Birth of Moses (2:1-4)

Note that each of Pharaoh's attempts to destroy Israel was countered by God's gift of prosperity and growth to Israelite families.

After each of Pharaoh's first three measures we read an almost doxological refrain: "The Israelites increased." God's final countermove is the most dramatic: Moses is born! God nullifies each step taken by Pharaoh to destroy Israel. Every ineffectual attempt to stop their birthrate is followed by an increase. Finally the potential hammer-blow to Egypt's power comes when Moses is born.

The Cosmic Battle

Sometimes we get immersed in the details of this dramatic story and miss the bigger picture, the struggle between the seed of the serpent and the seed of the woman. Pharaoh is the embodiment of the seed of the serpent and the Israelites embody the seed of the woman (see Gen. 3:15). God has promised to bring redemption through the seed of Abraham. The battle between Pharaoh and Israel in the first two chapters of Exodus is a cosmic one. Pharaoh's actions are part of the hell-bent determination of Satan to destroy the seed of the promise.

Seed of Serpent = Satan = Pharaoh as His Instrument
versus
Seed of Woman = God = Israel as His Instrument

In this cosmic battle Pharaoh's attempt to wipe out the people of God failed. This historical confrontation finds its New Testament parallel in Herod's attempt to destroy a generation of babies in Bethlehem (Matt. 2:16). Neither Pharaoh nor Herod can stand in the way of God's plan for his people.

Throughout history Satan has tried to prevent the increase of the church. Sometimes there is the frontal attack of political opposition that refuses to let a church evangelize. This has occurred in some communist and fascist countries. The people of God must pray and labor against this tool of Satan. "I urge . . . that . . . prayers [and] intercessions . . . be made for . . . kings and all those in authority, that we may live in all godliness and holiness" (1 Tim. 2:1, 2). The reason for such intercession is not just that we may enjoy contented and peaceful lives, but that the church might have the freedom to bring people to a saving knowledge of Christ. God "wants all men to be saved and to come to a knowledge of the truth" (1 Tim. 2:4).

At other times the opposition is more subtle. Neighbors mock or reject us because we seek to win others to Christ. When the church seeks to proclaim Christ in public arenas the secular forces often accuse Christians of breaking the principle of the separation of church and state. Christians are accused of being un-American when they demand laws that respect human life or restrain pornography. Clearly the church is to serve as the moral conscience of the public community. In all these areas and many more, the cosmic battles between Christ's kingdom and Satan's continue. The church of Christ, as was true of Israel, has the assurance that God will preserve and increase his people.

Satan is determined to bring spiritual genocide upon the people of God. But he cannot nullify God's promise. Our hope must be rooted in the one who conquers the Pharaohs and the Herods.

> The dragon stood in front of the woman who was about to give birth, so that he might devour her child the moment it was born. She gave birth to a son, a male child, who will rule all the nations with an iron scepter (Rev. 12:4, 5).

> Now have come the salvation and the power and the kingdom of our God, and the authority of his Christ. For the accuser of our brothers . . . has been hurled down.
> They overcame him by the blood of the Lamb and by the word of their testimony (Rev. 12:10, 11).

Note

1. Quoted by Jack Finegan in *Let My People Go: A Journey through Exodus* (Harper and Row, New York, 1963), 21.

Review Questions

1. What significant change took place in the name *Israel* in Exodus 1:1-9?

2. What was the hope of Israel? What is the hope of the Christian?

3. What is the cosmic battle that Exodus 1 and 2 describe?

Discussion Questions

1. What are the subtle ways in which the cosmic battle engages the people of God today?

2. How will your hope in the one who conquers the Pharaoh's and the Herods affect the way you act this week?

4

THEIR BONDAGE AND OURS

Biblical history is, in almost every instance, the out-working of the *word-and-act* pattern of biblical prophecy. God makes a promise, then acts in history to fulfill what he has promised. As we have seen, God has promised to make Abraham's children a nation of his people, and we can be sure that he will act to keep his promise. We will now look at his word of promise concerning bondage in Egypt and deliverance.

Israel's Bondage Foretold

Genesis 15:8-16 contains a dramatic vision given to Abram. It confirmed the certainty of the Lord's promise, though Abram was told that there would be an interim of bondage and slavery for his descendants before they possessed the land (vss 13, 14). In response to Abram's question, "O Sovereign LORD, how can I know that I will gain possession of [a land and offspring]?" (vs 8), Abram was instructed to take a heifer goat, a ram, a turtledove and a pigeon; and, except for the birds, to cut them in half. In the vision, Abram then saw a smoking firepot with a flaming torch pass between the pieces of the hewn animal. "On that day the LORD made a covenant with Abram" (Ex. 15:18).

In the human covenant-making of the Near East, the local sovereign commonly pledged his faithfulness to his promise by passing between the pieces of the hewn animal; it was a way of saying ceremonially, "If I do not keep my promise, may I be hewn in pieces like these animals!" This act was called an oath of self-malediction. In this dramatic scene God himself invoked the curse of self-malediction if his promise should prove false, passing between the hewn pieces in the form of a smoking firepot and a blazing torch (Gen. 15:17). By performing this ritual God declared that, if he failed his promise, he was to be slain like the animals and devoured.

The Lord's words of promise regarding future slavery related directly to the bondage in Egypt, and might be precisely why this word of revelation was accompanied by such an unusual appearance of the Lord. It would furnish much-needed understanding and encouragement during the dark days of Israel's servitude. Verses 13 and 14 briefly but clearly describe the years in Egypt. The word *strangers* used in this text — literally "sojourners" — does not speak merely of a negative experience, because it alludes to God's sustaining provision. However, after being sustained in Egypt and delivered from famine, Israel would experience enslavement and oppression. The exact method of the computation of the 400 years in Egypt poses a problem. It is probably a round number that is more precisely stated in Exodus 12:40 as 430 years.

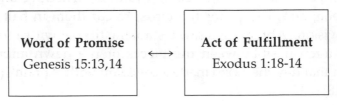

Word of Promise		Act of Fulfillment
Genesis 15:13,14	⟷	Exodus 1:18-14

This promise sets the whole bondage experience in the proper context of a biblical theology of history. God rules over world history, and in the course of time those nations that stand against his kingdom become ripe for his judgment. Furthermore, the central actors on the stage of world history are not the powers of Egypt or the Amorites but the people of God. History is not some mysterious riddle: God controls it for the purpose of establishing his kingdom. A sojourn and bondage for the people of God is one more step in his plan. Our response in the midst of much contemporary tribulation must be the faith of the patriarchs and the prayer of Jesus: "[Y]our kingdom come, your will be done on earth as it is in heaven" (Matt. 6:10).

The Bondage Intensifies

Nevertheless the Egyptians did enforce bondage and they did maintain very real and intense slavery. The bondage began in two cities whose exact identity and location have been lost in antiquity. But there is some evidence from archaeology that Pithom became a great center for building temples to solar worship and Raamses was a place for the worship of the Raamses pharaohs. An opulent and immense palace was built there from a factory "with ten tile molds of eight hundred different types."[1] This style seems to correspond to descriptions of Israelite work. Undoubtedly their artistry spread out from Pithom and Raamses. Even the materials of their labor — brick and mortar — are mentioned in Exodus 1:14. Certainly it was not some form of modern cement work, for such was unknown in the ancient world. The brick construction work of ancient Egypt used the sandy Nile clay, probably as an adhesive. The bricks were probably the sun-dried brick used in the treeless Nile valley. These basic construction materials comprised most of the architecture of ancient Egypt.

In Exodus 2:23, 24 we find a further description of Israel's bondage at the time one of the pharaohs (possibly Thutmose III) died. No doubt the death of an oppressive pharaoh would bring hope that the next ruler would be less oppressive. But nothing changed; indeed, things got worse. A cruel, heartless ruler, who may have been Amenhotep II, came to the throne. An inscription describes how he carried "seven Syrian leaders upside-down from the bow of his ship on the trip up the Nile, after which he personally sacrificed them."[2] From this cruel pharaoh would come such a persecution that the people "groaned and cried out" (Ex. 2:23). God, we are told, heard them and paid heed. All hope did not vanish, though the new king did nothing to encourage it. The Sovereign LORD of history heard the cry of his people "and was concerned about them" (2:25). Deliverance would not come from a king of Egypt but from the Lord himself.

In the midst of the confrontation between Moses and Pharaoh in Exodus 5 we have another vivid description of the severity of their bondage. The old flame of distrust came alive in Pharaoh because of Moses' demand to let the people go. So Pharaoh gave an order to two groups of people, the slave drivers and the foremen. The foremen were Israelites who were responsible to the slave drivers for the work done (vs 14). They were supposed to press their own people to fulfill each day's quota and implement Pharaoh's orders for the construction.

Straw was added to the sun-dried bricks of the Nile Valley to strengthen them and to increase their moldability.[3] Until now others had been gathering the straw and giving it to the brick-makers, but no more! Now they would have to gather the straw themselves, but with the same daily quotas. The burden of the work forced the Israelite foremen into the bold act of complaining to Pharaoh. They pointedly did not blame Pharaoh but called on him to arbitrate between them and the slave-masters. Not only did Pharaoh not change his mind but he reproached the Israelites for their laziness. As an excuse for his edict Pharaoh claimed that the Israelites wanted to go serve the Lord because they did not want to work. In effect the cruel Pharaoh was commanding, "Back to work, and meet your full quota while gathering your own straw."

Against such a background we can understand the negative response of Israel to Moses' words later on. They wouldn't listen to him because of their discouragement and cruel bondage (Ex. 6:9).

Egypt and the Antichrist

Can you imagine the fatigue, anger and frustration of the Israelites? Here was a foreign power that had for a time preserved them from the ravages of the famine but was now robbing them of their nationhood and personhood. They were nothing more than a bunch of slaves for the Egyptians. The theology of the exodus teaches us that Egypt is the symbol of worldly, anti-God power. The Egyptians were sensual (Ezek. 23:19-21) and marked by a pride that deserved the judgment of God. "This is what the Sovereign LORD says: 'I am against you, Pharaoh king of Egypt, you great monster lying among your streams. You say, "The Nile is mine; I made it for myself" ' " (Ezek. 29:3). It is not coincidental that any future alliance with later Israelite history is considered a "covenant with death, an agreement with the grave" (Is. 28:15). Egypt becomes a vivid symbol of sin and the subsequent bondage and death that it brings.

The book of Revelation confirms the symbolism and typology of Egypt. The figurative language of Revelation 11:8 presents two witnesses who had power to stop the rains (Elijah) and bring the plagues (Moses). But the beast (Satan and his representatives) comes out of the Abyss and kills them. The great city where they are killed is "figuratively called Sodom and Egypt." The same power, figuratively speaking, crucified Jesus Christ. For a short time, as the Lord marks time, peoples of many nations and races will gloat over the folly of these witnesses, but eventually by the breath of the Lord they will be resurrected and given victory over their enemies. Clearly Egypt is the symbol of opposition to the plans and purposes of God's redemptive work. Egypt is a type of the Antichrist that destroys the earth and seeks to enslave the people of God.

This biblical symbolism provides the background for Jesus' words to the "children of Abraham" in John 8:31-41. He had said to the Jews who had professed faith in him, "If you hold to my teaching, you are really my disciples. Then you will know the truth, and the truth will set you free" (John 8:31, 32). Their response was, "We have . . . never been slaves of anyone." Can you recognize the irony of these words in light of the national roots in Egyptian slavery of his hearers? Jesus then teaches them that all sinners are enslaved in their sin. It is only when the Redeemer sets you free that you are truly free.

Humankind stands as a race of free moral agents before God, but John 8 teaches that we have lost the moral power to determine the direction of our lives. We have an innate bias toward evil and are not able to apprehend the love of God. We are totally unable to seek and to do spiritual things, the things that pertain to salvation. In terms of biblical doctrine, this condition is often called "total inability." By virtue of our slavery in sin, we cannot save or deliver ourselves. The symbolism of Egyptian slavery also reminds us that we are not only in bondage to spiritual death but also in subjection to the power of physical death dragging us into the grave. We too need an exodus! We cannot be saved from the power and enslavement of *our* Egypt apart from the supernatural renewing and resurrecting power of a redeemer.

It is important that we relate this biblical symbolism of a worldly, anti-God power to our individual lives as the people of God. Our modern secular world leaves God out and seeks in subtle, but nevertheless clear, terms to enslave us to the world. Today these passages speak not to those who labor in bricks and mortar but to those who are caught up in the rat race of modern business life, driven by the taskmaster's whip which insists that we provide modern luxuries and gadgets as essentials to life. Are even the people of God enslaved by a worldly, anti-God power? What are some modern evidences of this subtle enslavement?

These passages also challenge our corporate lives as the people of God. Here were God's people living in the midst of a non-Christian social and governmental system. Sometimes, in God's overruling providence, it was a source of blessing. They had experienced the hospitality and provision of the Egyptians in their initial years in Egypt. Joseph, one of their own, had risen to a place of power and prestige. But a time of peace and prosperity (Ex. 1:1-7) seems to have led them to settle down in Egypt. They had begun to worship the Egyptian gods and to enjoy the luxuries of Egypt. But now Pharaoh had become the oppressor. They were no longer experiencing the comfort and provision of Egypt, only its bondage. What had once been an instrument of physical blessing and sustenance was now the instrument of oppression.

Are there evidences of the oppression of God's people by the state today? For example: Is it possible that we are enslaved by the popular understanding that the First Amendment to the United States Constitution holds that religion and politics, or religion and education, do not and should not mix? The amendment states, "Congress shall make no law respecting an establishment of religion or prohibiting the free exercise thereof or abridging the freedom of speech . . . " Most of our popular, secular society would interpret these words to mean that any attempt to apply God's word to such public legal issues as abortion or pornography is an infringement of First Amendment rights. Thus there is an attempt to rob the church of its freedom to speak for and support legislation concerning public moral issues. Are we being enslaved by this secular mentality?

The assumption has also been made that the state has the primary responsibility for the education of children. The judicial system's failure to recognize that a presumed neutrality toward the study of academic subjects in school is really secularism, and the result is the oppression of Christian students. Current practice results in God's being left out of his own world! Doesn't such a position on the part of many in public education really *establish* the *religion* of secularism? Should believers ask public educational systems to give equal time, or even *some* time, for the presentation of a Christian world-and-life view in what public officials *claim* is a pluralistic educational system? Are the secular systems robbing us of our freedom to go out into God's world and serve him in every area of our lives?

Are there places in our society where we should be saying through public witness to the enslaving powers of this world, "God says, 'Let my people go!'—that they may serve him"?

Notes

1. Charles Aling, *Egypt and Bible History* (Grand Rapids: Baker Book House, 1981), 69.

2. Quoted in W. H. Gispen, "Exodus," *Bible Student's Commentary* (Grand Rapids: Zondervan, 1982), 48.

3. A. Lucas and J. R. Harris, *Ancient Egyptian Materials and Industries*, 4th ed. (London: Edwards Arnold, 1962), 74, 75.

Review Questions

1. Where in Genesis is Israel's bondage foretold?

2. How is Egypt a type of the Antichrist?

3. How is Israel a type of the Christian?

Discussion Questions

1. What encouragement can we gain from Israel's tribulation experience?

2. How would you respond to someone who says, "The exodus means nothing to me; I've never been enslaved to anyone"?

5

MOSES: INSTRUMENT OF HOPE

The wrenching hopelessness of slavery and oppression! Was there any hope? Would God act? Yes, even in the midst of Israel's slavery and degradation, God had already begun to prepare for the deliverance of his people. In the plan of God a baby was born who would grow up to be God's appointed leader for the exodus. Because of Pharaoh's decree to kill all the Israelite male children (Ex. 1:22) Moses' mother concealed her baby for three months until she could no longer hide him. His parents demonstrated fearlessness and faith in God's grace and provision. Hebrews 11:23 comments: "By faith Moses' parents hid him for three months after he was born, because they saw he was no ordinary child, and they were not afraid of the king's edict."

God's Provision

The romantic story of a hiding place on a tributary of the Nile and the preparation of his papyrus basket or ark (Ex. 2:3) is one of the best-known stories in the Bible. Moses' sister Miriam stayed by the little baby to care for him. What appeared at first to be an imminent disaster, the appearance of Pharaoh's daughter to bathe at that very spot, turned out to be the means by which God prepared Moses for his adult leadership role. Pharaoh's daughter saw the child, had compassion on him and made arrangements for him to have a nurse — his own mother.

We may know who this princess was. It is likely that Moses was born when the pharaoh had only one living daughter. If the pharaoh was Thutmose I, his daughter, the famous Hatshepsut, was that princess. Thutmose had no son of his own, which may explain why Moses was adopted. It was also common to adopt a son from a conquered city, bring him to the capital of Thebes and train him in the ways and loyalties of Egypt. The adopted son would then be sent back to rule his native kingdom for Egypt. Perhaps Moses was trained to keep the Israelites loyal to Pharaoh!

Notice God's marvelous dual provision: first, Moses' own mother to provide him with his early training and bonding to his own family and people; later, instruction in the wisdom of Egypt. There is a gap of at least several months (perhaps more than a year) between "[T]he woman took the baby and nursed him" (vs 9) and "When the child grew older she took him to Pharaoh's daughter and he became her son" (vs 10). In the Exodus narrative we are told little of the intervening years, but the words of Stephen in Acts 7:22 are an apt summary: "Moses was educated in all the wisdom of the Egyptians." The enemies of Israel provided Moses with the very tools he would need to bring about Israel's deliverance. Recent archaeological findings give us some insight into Moses' education. He would have been instructed in theology, astronomy, medicine, languages and mathematics. Moses had all the privileges and education of the royal household.

Moses Identifies with His People

The "One day" of Exodus 2:11 takes us forty years beyond the events described in verses 1-10. Moses had left the palace to watch, as an interested observer, the cruel oppression of one of his Israelite brethren. He saw with emotion this act of cruelty and killed the Egyptian. Hebrews 11:25 tells us that, by the act of killing the Egyptian, Moses made a decision "to be mistreated along with the people of God rather than enjoy the pleasures of sin for a short time." Was the act of killing wrong? Though Moses was acting on behalf of his people we must say yes, because he had no right to act as judge. Acts 7:25 makes it plain that he already had some realization that God would use him to rescue the people of God, but in killing the Egyptian taskmaster he demonstrated a lack of patience to wait for God's call to action.

Moses' subsequent intervention in a conflict between two Hebrews elicited this response from the guilty man: "Are you thinking of killing me as you killed the Egyptian?" (Ex. 2:14). It was clear that his deed of murder was known, and Moses fled when he heard that Pharaoh intended to execute him. It is likely that this act of identification with the Israelites occurred near the time of Hatshepsut's death. We know that her husband, who lived a frustrated life in the background while she ruled, sought every means to remove all memory of her, and any excuse to kill her favorites.

What would now become of all the training in Egypt? The man who in Egypt was robed like royalty would now climb the boulders of Midian and work for his father-in-law. But this was no pointless detour in Moses' life. Be-

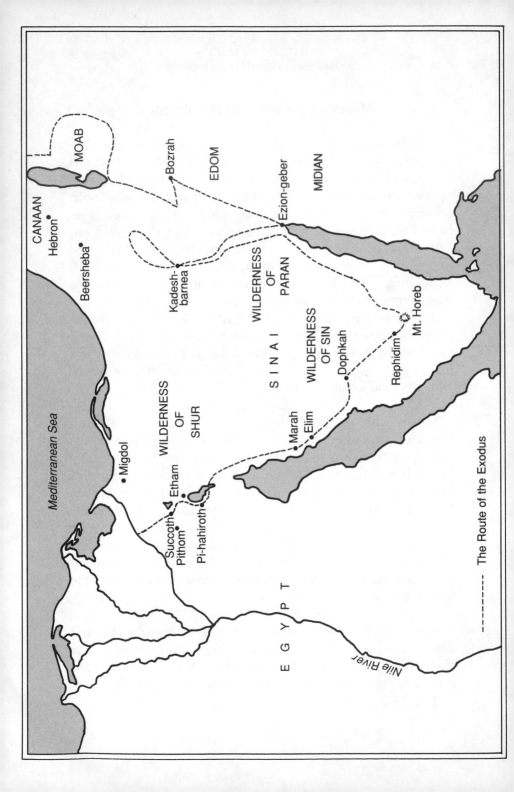

cause Midian was located to the south and east of Canaan, Moses was settled in a land strategically located between Canaan and Egypt. The wilderness of Midian served as a training ground to prepare Moses to lead his people.

Moses might have used his position in Egypt to bring freedom and deliverance to Israel. In the plan and purpose of God, he did not. If Moses had used his political position or bargained his authority for Israel's release, deliverance would have been by political power. The deliverance would have focused on a man and his cunning and position. Instead the narrative dramatically emphasizes that God is the deliverer and Moses is merely his instrument. "I have come down to rescue them from the hand of the Egyptians" (Ex. 3:8) is the word that Moses is to bring from God to the Israelites.

The Burning Bush

It was probably during the time that Moses was in the land of Midian that Thutmose was conducting military campaigns against Palestine and Syria. Notice how God prepared the way for Israel by using Egypt to weaken the inhabitants of Palestine. The pharaoh then died (Ex. 2:23), but his death made no difference in the severe bondage of Israel. God heard the sighs and groans of Israel, and as we see in Exodus 2 the setting of his call to Moses can be found in the words, "[H]e remembered his covenant with Abraham, with Isaac and with Jacob" (vs 24). Tending the sheep, Moses saw the wonderful and incredible sight of a bush aflame yet never consumed. God told Moses to take his shoes off his feet, for he was on holy ground. He revealed that he was the God of Abraham, Isaac and Jacob and that he had heard the groaning of his people.

Since many of the Israelites had forgotten God, how would Moses make him known to Israel? God responded to Moses' question by revealing his name: "I AM WHO I AM" (3:14). God declared in this significant expression that he is not shaped by man's speculations and formulations: he is precisely who he is. He does what he pleases. He is the God of the covenant and as such he remains the same. Long ago he had told Abraham that he would bring his people out of Egypt; now he is about to make good on that promise. The name associated with this revelation is *Yahweh*, sometimes translated "Jehovah" or "LORD."

The modesty of Moses in Exodus 3:11-4:17 reminds us that the coming redemption will be accomplished entirely by God and not by the people or Moses. Instead of a rash willingness to deliver the people, Moses is now afraid to undertake such a job even in the Lord's strength. Though there is a certain rebelliousness against the Lord's call in Moses' repeated excuses, his response also directs our attention to the Lord's strength. It is God who gives Moses his brother Aaron to go with him as his spokesman. It is the Lord who gives him the three miraculous signs to show to the people and to Pharaoh. The Lord's final restatement of Moses' assignment (4:14-17) has a note of anger in it. The road to the exodus was fraught with opposition, even from within the house of Israel. It would take supernatural and cataclysmic acts of God to bring about this deliverance.

As we study this passage we must not overlook some of its unique aspects of revelation. The last time the Lord had appeared to a human being was in a vision to Jacob before he came to Egypt (Gen. 46:2-4). At that time God promised that Jacob's descendants would be a great nation. That had been centuries ago. Now, with the existence of the nation at a critical point, he appears again, this time in a direct and personal way.

We should note also that this appearance occurs at Mount Horeb, the mountain of God (Ex. 3:1). *Horeb* and *Sinai* are two names for the same mountain. This mountain will be the place where God frequently meets with his people. In the burning bush there may well be a deliberate allusion to Genesis 3:24 and the angels who guard with flaming swords the way into the presence of the Lord. Fire is frequently the symbol of the Lord's presence, as when he descends on Sinai and when he protects in the form of a pillar of fire (Ex. 13:21). The symbolism probably lies in both the destructive and the purifying effects of fire. Normally fire speaks of God's presence, holiness, and anger toward sin (Ex. 19:18; 32:10).

Moses is a great example of faith and obedience. He was willing to leave all the wealth and power of Egypt to identify with slaves. But as we have seen, he also serves as a negative example. Moses produced a series of excuses to avoid the Lord's call. He should have responded with instant submission and trusted God's gifts and grace for his strength. Yet Moses serves as more than just an example. He is called out onto the stage of redemptive history to play an important role as the liberator of God's people. Thus he has a prominent place in all of Old Testament revelation. In the book of Hosea we read, "The LORD used a prophet to bring Israel up from Egypt" (Hos. 12:13).

Further, when we place Moses' life within the total context of Scripture we find that he is central to its pattern of promise and fulfillment. His life is instrumental in the fulfillment of much of God's promise to Abraham that Israel would be a great nation, receive a land and be a blessing to the world. When we look back to those promises we see that Moses was the means of their fulfillment, at least in their external and physical form. Under Moses Israel became a great nation and received national identity and coherence. He also brought them to the border of the promised land. Moreover, before Israel could be a blessing to the world they had to experience, both in their personal and their national life-patterns, between paganism and belief in the God of the covenant. The conflict between Israel and Egypt was ultimately a contest between false gods and the true God of Israel. Seeing the sharp distinction between the gods of Egypt and the Lord God was essential before Israel could be a source of blessing to the world.

Moses is also a key figure in the pattern of promise and fulfillment when we look forward in the flow of Old Testament revelation. Moses does not just stand at the beginning of a succession of prophets, he sets the standard for the rest: "I will raise up for them a prophet like you from among their brothers" (Deut. 18:18). In addition Moses essentially became the ruler over all God's house. In the NIV translation of Numbers 12:7 the Lord says of him, "[H]e is faithful in all my house." But it might better be translated "[H]e is set over all my house." This expression establishes Moses as a figure who points to a great fulfillment in the New Testament. He is the Old Testament redeemer.

The close tie between the words and deeds of God — his revelation and his redemptive actions in history, so typical of God's relationship with Moses—will not appear again in Scripture with such intensity until the life and ministry of Jesus Christ. Moses' meeting God at the burning bush and at Sinai, and his delivering of God's word to the people, are unique events. Nowhere else in the Old Testament is the word of promise fulfilled as immediately as it is in God's redemption through the exodus. And, as Christ's would later be, the redemptive acts and the signs of Moses' authority were miraculous. The central purpose of the miracles was to confirm the authority of God's messenger and prophet and to point to the source of the power (Ex. 4:1-10). The closeness with which these three elements are linked — revelation given, redemption accomplished and miraculous authority — will not appear again until the coming of Jesus Christ.

Prophet, Priest and King

The fullness of Moses' position as a type or forerunner of Christ is best seen in terms of the three offices of Christ, who accomplished his saving work in his threefold ministry as prophet, priest and king. We see Moses also fulfilling these three roles, though incompletely and imperfectly.

At the burning bush and at Sinai, Moses the prophet received the word from the Lord and was called to communicate it to the people. The prophet like Moses who was foretold in Deuteronomy 18:15 was none other than Jesus Christ. On several occasions Moses acted as a priest prior to the institution of the Aaronic priesthood: "He got up early the next morning and built an altar at the foot of the mountain" (Ex. 24:4). Our Lord referred to this event when he instituted the new covenant and its ceremony in the Lord's Supper (Luke 22:1-20). The preeminent example of Moses' priestly office occurred when he offered his life as a vicarious sacrifice for the sin of the people after they built the golden calf (Ex. 32:30-33). Was Moses a king? Yahweh alone was king in the exodus; but through leadership and legislation Moses typified the royal office of Jesus Christ.

This marvelous background enables us to read the glorious statement of the book of Hebrews in fuller biblical perspective. The beauty of our Savior and the fullness of his person and work shine out even more brightly in this context: "Therefore, holy brothers, who share in the heavenly calling, fix your thoughts on Jesus, the apostle and high priest whom we confess. He was faithful to the one who appointed him, just as Moses was faithful in all God's house. Jesus has been found worthy of greater honor than Moses, just as the builder of a house has greater honor than the house itself. For every house is built by someone, but God is the builder of everything. Moses was faithful as a servant in all God's house, testifying to what would be said in the future. But Christ is faithful as a son over God's house. And we are his house, if we hold on to our courage and the hope of which we boast" (Heb. 3:1-6).

Moses (Type)	Christ (Fulfillment)
Prophet: Deuteronomy 18:18, 19 ⟷	Prophet: Hebrews 1:1-14
Priest: Exodus 24:4 ⟷	Priest: Luke 22.20
King: Deuteronomy 18:18 ⟷	King

So Moses is more than just a good example. His relationship to the people of Israel determined their relationship to God. The application to our lives of the exodus story and the wilderness wandering is no mere spiritual abstraction when we realize that the relationship of Israel to Moses parallels the relationship of the believer to Christ. Paul precisely emphasizes this in 1 Corinthians 10:1, 2: "[O]ur forefathers were all under the cloud and . . . they all passed through the sea. They were all baptized into Moses in the cloud and in the sea." Baptism establishes a personal relationship between Christ and the believer on the basis of Christ's redemptive work, so the mighty act of exodus by the hand of Moses pledged Israel to faith in him. Have you wondered why rebellion against Moses was treated so harshly? It is because rebellion against Moses was comparable to rebellion against Christ. In the light of this truth the exodus and the wilderness wanderings are a great drama of mixed faith and unbelief.

The raising up of Moses as God's redeemer reminds us of the sovereignty of the Lord's grace. That reminder was dramatic when he was preserved in the reeds and humbled in Midian. Salvation comes not by human power or position but by the servant preserved and called by God. The deliverance from our bondage comes not by our own efforts but by the grace and power of God. He is the great I AM, the one who keeps covenant and who is known by his acts and revelation. We owe our life and hope to the God of the exodus, who is the God and Father of our Lord Jesus Christ. God is no abstraction: he establishes a relationship with his people. In this context Yahweh is simply shorthand for all God's dealings of grace. All of these acts and revelation comprise deep theological truth, but they also call for the response of faith: "See to it, brothers, that none of you has a sinful, unbelieving heart that turns away from the living God" (Heb. 3:12).

Review Questions

1. What was God's dual provision to the baby Moses?

2. How did Moses identify with the Israelites?

3. How is Moses prominent in the Old Testament? How does he point to the New?

Discussion Questions

1. God could have used Moses' position of influence to negotiate Israel's freedom. Why didn't he?

2. In response to Moses' modesty God promised to provide fully for him. How has God fulfilled that promise in *our* lives? What ought to be our response?

6

REDEMPTION FROM EGYPT

Words are a precious commodity. Without them there can be no fully developed interpersonal relationships. Without them we have an incomplete revelation from God. Yet our Christian vocabulary often becomes hackneyed, repetitive and meaningless. Sometimes we use a biblical word or term without seeking to comprehend its full meaning. This can lead to a trite vocabulary and a less-than-faithful witness. Our Bible study can be enriched by the understanding of words in their full biblical context. That leads not only to enriched Bible study but to a greater knowledge of God and a more-faithful witness. As we have seen, words and acts go together in the Bible.

A central biblical word is *redemption*. It denotes the means by which salvation is achieved and includes deliverance and the payment of a ransom. The Bible speaks of the exodus as a redemption: "I am the LORD, and I will bring you out from under the yoke of the Egyptians. I will free you from being slaves to them, and will redeem you with an outstretched arm and with mighty acts of judgment" (Ex. 6:6, 7). The great act of God in the exodus is the foundation of our understanding of redemption. The ultimate root of our redemption in Christ is found in this historical event.

Redemption is also a word that marks the life story of Israel. The exodus stands out as the most important mighty act of God until the coming of Jesus Christ. It even has pride of place over creation. The Old Testament always assumes that its greatest theme is that Israel's God is the God of salvation and redemption. It is by this mighty deed that Israel came to know God as the God of compassion and saving power. Therefore it is upon this mighty act that the nation depended for its very existence. As we have seen in previous chapters, the exodus gave substance to the hopes of Abraham. Further, it is the origin of the nation over which King David would rule. Thus the exodus is the watershed event of the Old Testament. All that comes after it builds upon this great redemptive event. From the covenant originating in the exodus and instituted at Sinai the people of God look forward to a new covenant and a fulfilled redemption in Jesus Christ. Israel's statement of faith, often repeated in their worship and everyday life from this time on, would be "God's people brought out of Egypt." Other articles of faith would be added but this basic article would remain the same.

God Promises Redemption

At the end of Exodus 5 Moses showed that he was a temporal redeemer. He was a sinner and protested because God had not yet kept his promise. Israel was not just unredeemed: they were trapped in bondage, both objectively and subjectively. Their own inability to serve the Lord in the fullness of their life was emotionally and spiritually destructive. But Exodus 6 contains a startling statement calculated to encourage Israel. Pharaoh will not just let them go—he will *expel* them.

The God who will act in such a way must be a God of character, so words relate not only to our understanding of what God *does* but also who God s as our redeemer. Verse 3 tells us that Abraham, Isaac and Jacob did not know the name *Yahweh* even though it was as Yahweh that God had spoken to them (e.g., Gen. 12:1, 4; 17:1; 18:1). The exodus brought new content to the revelation of God, so these Israelites had an advantage over the patriarchs — a fuller and greater revelation.

God had not forgotten his promise, and he fully intended to carry it out. So Moses was called to address Israel on God's behalf. Can you spot the three points of his sermon (Ex. 6:6-8)? First, he reminded them that God was the LORD and would redeem them. Second, he said that they would be redeemed by a mighty hand and by mighty acts of judgment. The third proclamation on behalf of the Lord was the vital one: he would adopt Israel to be his own. From now on God would not only look on Israel as his own but would also establish a relationship with them, a relationship based not only upon their emergence from the misery of Egypt but also upon his making them his people.

Moses relayed this message to Israel. You might expect tremendous response such as, "Let's go claim the victory of the Lord!" Instead they were so discouraged under the bondage that they could not hear the message. They had heard it before and God had not acted. The church — New Testament Israel — often fails to hear God's prophecy. Today in the midst of our bondage God says, "You are my people." But we are impatient, discouraged. Both the burden of satanic influence and our lack of faith cause us to turn a deaf ear to his word.

Having discovered his inadequacy with his own people (Ex. 5:22, 23), Moses demurred at the thought of confronting Pharaoh. Despite the Lord's anger over his earlier reluctance to accept leadership of God's people (4:14) and the guarantee in Exodus 6:1 that the mighty hand of God would bring the exodus to a successful end, Moses is still slow to obey. Sadly, the church in our own time has not been immune to discouragement and ineffectiveness because the people of God have been slow to trust that God will bring to pass what he has promised!

Suddenly there is a break in the main story. Verses 14-27 give a long genealogy that identifies Moses' lineage. It is a typically Hebraic way of saying that Moses and Aaron are legitimate. From founding father Reuben up to Levi it reminds the Israelites of priestly connections and roots. The people of God still have their roots. We may be forgotten by our future generations, when nothing is left but names, registers of births, marriages, deaths. But these genealogies remind us of both the faithfulness of God and the fact that he never forgets his people.

God Is in Control

Exodus 6:28-30 begins with the repetition of Exodus 6:10, 11, indicating that a new section of the story is beginning. Moses, who is about to relate the mighty acts of God, repeats his conviction that he is an inadequate instrument of God. This human redeemer is no larger-than-life hero. It is through weak instruments that God makes his glory known. God's great purpose was that the pharaoh should know that "I am the LORD" (6:29). *Yahweh* is used not only as a title of authentication and guarantee of a command but also to explain the reason for the command. "I am

Yahweh, therefore you must do it. I keep my word of covenant, therefore you must do as I say" (cf Lev. 19:18).

Because of the inadequacy of Moses, God appointed Aaron to serve as the middleman between Moses and Pharaoh. Up to this point Moses was the one who spoke to Pharaoh; now Aaron becomes his mouthpiece. Moses has been invested with divine authority over Pharaoh, and Aaron is his prophet. The New Testament reminds us that when we act in the name of Jesus and under his authority we are his representatives. In Chapter 5 of this textbook we suggested the unique and authoritative role of Moses. But rather than hearing and responding to God's word, Pharaoh would harden his heart. In this passage we read that God would harden Pharaoh's heart (7:3). How could a loving God harden someone's heart? It is not a reference to something that God merely foreknows but something that he will bring about. It is the repetition of something already told Moses in Exodus 4:21. This is one of those clear illustrations in the Bible of God's absolute sovereignty. Nothing occurs apart from his control and purpose, yet human beings are held responsible for their acts. The ultimate cause is God, but Pharaoh's hardened heart is blamed on himself. You say, here is an evident contradiction! Yes, but a contradiction to the limited minds of humans, not to God. The multiplying of signs and wonders emphasizes the fact that the hardening of Pharaoh's heart had one ultimate purpose: the manifesting of the glory and omnipotence of God.

The sovereignty of God is the source of our hope, since even the evil in the world accomplishes his purpose. God accomplishes his will even through the hard-hearted sinfulness of human beings. Sinful people are responsible for their sin, but in the inscrutable wisdom of God he uses even that sin to accomplish his ultimate purpose. What folly that some people think, like Pharaoh, that they can thwart the plans of God by their stubborn rebellion. He rules and overrules for his glory.

Because of God's sovereign control, Israel is the Lord's army and is therefore called "my divisions" (7:4), a term with a military connotation. What a remarkable expression for these oppressed people! They were the army of the Lord because they were in the right and Pharaoh was in the wrong. What metaphor do you think most aptly applies to the people of God: hospital, army, fortress? Notice the number of times in the Bible that the people of God are described as an army (cf Eph. 6:10-18). As God's people we need to be more aware today of the spiritual battle. Because our conflict is spiritual we often fail to realize its seriousness. The opposition to the church by secular and humanistic forces is no less real than the conflict between Israel and Egypt.

Miraculous Signs and Wonders

In this confrontation God executed his plan through miracles. The miraculous served to demonstrate the power and authority of Yahweh in contrast to the pagan gods. Magic flourished in pagan Egypt, but Egyptian magic was different from magic today: Egyptians believed that one could manipulate one's gods. Since Egypt's gods were the forces behind nature, magic was an attempt to influence the gods. Later Scripture even identifies two of these ma-
ates their confrontation with Moses to our
itual battle as the New Israel (2 Timothy
Pharaoh asked for a miracle, Moses was to

tell Aaron to cast down his staff and it would become a snake. God's staff, carried by the mediator, Moses, was intended for use in leading Israel. It was the symbol of authority. Furthermore one of the central purposes of miracles was to confirm the authority of the prophet. Pharaoh summoned his wise men, sorcerers and magicians. By their magic and secret arts they were able to duplicate the miracle.

Was this a manifestation of satanic power, especially since Moses and Aaron were pleading for the release of Israel (the seed of the woman, Gen. 3:15, Rev. 12:13-15)? Egyptian magic commonly practiced snake charming either by some manipulation of the animal or by sleight of hand. Bible scholars disagree about the nature and power of the magic of the Egyptians. Whether by sleight of hand, animal manipulation or directly by the power of the evil one, the practice served Satan's purposes. Pharaoh was not led to repentance by seeing the staffs of his magicians devoured. He was stubborn in his unbelief.

The story of the plagues follows. It is so well-known that we are apt to overlook the fact that the plagues constituted a contest between Israel and Egypt, between God and the gods. There will be a more detailed study of that contest in the next chapter. We often have difficulty seeing historical portions of Scripture as relevant and applicable to our lives, because we think only of personal and moralistic applications. But the doctrinal application of these events is significant for the Christian life. The Old Testament believer is linked to us by virtue of an historical redemptive act of God. There is an inseparable link between the historic facts and the practice of religious life. That is why the Ten Commandments open with a reference to the redemptive act of the exodus (Ex. 20:2). The redemption from Egypt provides the motive for obedience. As late as Isaiah the people are called to look back to the ultimate root of their calling and life in the exodus (Is. 51:2).

So the exodus deliverance provides us with some biblical principles that will appear in future deliverances and enable us to see the glory and fullness of our deliverance in Christ. The people of God in both the Old and New Testaments must be gripped by these principles because they become both the source of our gratitude and our motive for obedience. Godly obedience is rooted in redemption and grows from that root.

What principles about redemption can we learn from the plagues?

First, that redemption is a deliverance from an objective kingdom of sin and evil. We usually individualize and internalize sin. Indeed sin does have expression in persons and in their hearts; but the Egyptian power is a manifestation of a kingdom of wickedness. What enslaved Israel was not merely political or physical bondage but satanic power opposed to the kingdom of God. The hardening of Pharaoh's heart reveals the nature of the opposition. The kingdom of sin stands in opposition to the kingdom of righteousness. There is demonic activity in the background of the story: the actors are not merely Egyptians but Egyptian gods and magicians. There was and is a subjective side to this evil as well. Israel was about to be delivered not just from objective bondage but from inward iption. Though the Israelites had not come e knowledge of Yahweh they had served t (Josh. 24:14). Furthermore the history of the wilderness wanderings, with Israel's turning to golden calves and repeated longings to return to Egypt, seem to demonstrate that they had been corrupted in Egypt both in their hearts and by the conduct of their lives.

Second, the deliverance emphasizes God's sovereignty in redemption. From Moses' hesitation to accept his assignment to the hardness of Pharaoh's heart, the narrative of Exodus 4-7 prepares us to see the power of the Lord. Deliverance comes not by the permission of Pharaoh or by the talents of Moses, but by the Lord in order to demonstrate his sovereignty. Through Moses he said to Pharaoh, "I have raised you up for this very purpose, that I might show you my power and that my name might be proclaimed in all the earth" (Ex. 9:16). But in quoting this verse in Romans 9:17 the apostle Paul is quick to add in verse 18, "Therefore God has mercy on whom he wants to have mercy, and he hardens whom he wants to harden." Whether for judgment or for mercy, then, the power of God is there to carry out the will of God.

The great theme of all of Scripture is that God chooses us to become his people by his omnipotent work of redemption, carried out in history and applied to our lives. What a reason for gratitude, what a motive for obedience!

> What if he did this to make the riches of his glory known to the objects of his mercy, whom he prepared in advance for glory — even us, whom he also called, not only from the Jews but also from the Gentiles? As he says in Hosea:

"I will call them 'my people' who are not my people;
   and I will call her 'my loved one' who is not my
   loved one . . . "

It is just as Isaiah said previously:

"Unless the Lord Almighty had left us descendants,
   we would have become like Sodom, we would have
   been like Gomorrah" (Rom. 9:23-25, 29).

We might interpret Romans 9 in the light of the exodus as follows: People today can become "like Egypt" — hardhearted rebels against the kingdom of God. Only the sovereign mercy and grace of God redeems us from such a condition.

Review Questions

1. Define *redemption*.

2. What principles about redemption are found in the plagues?

Discussion Questions

1. What advantage did the Israelites have over the patriarchs? What advantage do we have over the Israelites?

2. What discouragements prevent us from hearing the message of God today?

3. How does God make his glory known through weak instruments today?

7

THE LORD OF JUDGMENT

Moses came into the court of Pharaoh as he had years before. He stood before Pharaoh, but this time he came not to ask a favor or to plead his adoptive position. He did not even beg Pharaoh to be more kind to the Israelite people. Instead he spoke for God and said, "Let my people go that they may serve me." Pharaoh responded in anger: "Who is this Yahweh? I will not let Israel go." He made the labor of the Israelites even more burdensome. They were commanded to gather their own straw while continuing to produce the same daily allotment of brick as before. The Hebrew officers who supervised the people were beaten because they failed to meet their quota. The officers complained to Moses that his pleas to Pharaoh had made their task harder. Moses brought their complaint to God and received assurance that the Lord would deliver his people.

The next time, Aaron went with Moses to Pharaoh. When Moses told his brother to cast his staff down it became a snake. Pharaoh called his wise men, sorcerers and magicians, who were able to imitate the miracle; but Aaron's staff swallowed up the staffs of the magicians. In spite of this dramatic display of the Lord's authority "Pharaoh's heart [was] unyielding" (Ex. 7:14). This incident became the context for the plagues that were God's judgment both on hard-hearted Pharaoh and on Egypt.

God's Judgment: The Plagues

Did the plagues really happen? Are there any Egyptian records that confirm them? There are no such records, which would appear to be a cause for embarrassment to Bible-believing Christians. The reason that there are no records, however, gives us an important understanding of the plagues. The Egyptians kept historical records in order to impress their gods. Records of disasters would not enhance the reputation of the Egyptians in the eyes of either their gods or their enemies.

The plagues occur under the sovereign redemptive purpose of God. In commissioning Moses, God had told him that deliverance from Egypt would come only by the supreme power of God overcoming the might of Pharaoh. He and Egypt would be smitten with wonders or signs from God: "But I know that the king of Egypt will not let you go unless a mighty hand compels him. So I will stretch out my hand and strike the Egyptians with all the wonders that I will perform among them. After that, he will let you go" (Ex. 3:19, 20). So God had promised that he would smite Egypt with all his wonders. The plagues are described by a Hebrew word meaning "blow" or "stroke" as well as "wonder" and "signs." These words underline their twofold purpose: God's sovereign activity both in salvation and in judgment against Pharaoh. The devouring of the staffs of the Egyptian magicians by Aaron's staff includes this judgment motif. The story is a description of power against power. What a contest! Would Egyptian might prevail and frustrate the Lord's purpose? The disasters demonstrate the wrath of God against his enemy, Egypt.

Notice how salvation and judgment are linked. What was wrath for the Egyptians was God's salvation to the Israelites. Paul refers to this in Romans 9:22, 23: "What if God, choosing to show his wrath and make his power known, bore with great patience the objects of his wrath — prepared for destruction? What if he did this to make the riches of his glory known to the objects of his mercy[?]" For the unbelieving Egyptian it was God's justice manifest even in the judicial hardening of Pharaoh's heart. Left to himself he would have refused the overture of salvation. But for the believer the plagues were acts of deliverance. They reveal the accomplishment of the loving purpose of God (Rom. 8:28, 29). Throughout Scripture we see that salvation must come by judgment. The judgment meted out to Jesus Christ results in the ultimate victory that overcomes the world. By means of the crucifixion Jesus bore the judgment of God on behalf of his people and thus delivers them from both the enemy and the wrath of God.

So a new stage in Israel's liberation was about to commence. All the Egyptians were brought under God's punitive judgment. The significance and relevance of the plagues can be seen when we realize that at issue here were not such questions as how the Egyptian magicians could have reproduced the miracles of Moses. Rather there is a genuine conflict of power. The contest focuses on the power of Egypt versus the power of God. Often Egypt's power was a fraud because the gods of Egypt are impotent.

Some interpretations of these passages focus on Pharaoh's psychological response to Moses and Aaron. But the reference to Moses' boldness or even to Pharaoh's hard heart is not a psychological matter. Pharaoh willfully refused to listen and God judicially abandoned him. The unifying theme is the demand of Moses that his people be released from Pharaoh's servitude to serve the Lord (7:16; 8:1), not a psychological contest between two men. The plagues were brought on Egypt in order that Pharaoh might know that Yahweh is God (7:17; 10:2), that he is unique, that he is God in Egypt (8:22), that Pharaoh might learn the power and the name of the Lord (9:16) and that the earth belongs to him (9:29).

Therefore the contest developed between Yahweh and his servant Moses on the one hand and the gods of Egypt and their servant Pharaoh on the other. Pharaoh had already revealed his own defiance: "Who is the LORD, that I should obey him?" (5:2). A mortal struggle developed that, as we have seen, was forecast in Genesis 3, where the people of God (the woman and her seed) and the people of Satan (the serpent and its heirs) are locked in a titanic struggle. This total war is characterized by the total involvement of the combatants. The enemy is prejudiced, filled with hatred and irrationality. In its attempts to succeed it is willing even to lose face. Humanly speaking, Pharaoh had the superior forces and the advantage was heavily weighted in his favor. But when Yahweh acted in accord with his promise the kingdom of God prevailed and the kingdom of this world experienced humiliating defeat. In the same way Revelation 4 reiterates these struggles in an exodus-plague motif. Scenes are set sometimes in the camp of the enemy, sometimes in the camp of the saints. Two kingdoms are in conflict; but water turned to blood, boils, hail, locusts and darkness are the arsenal of God. Thus the story of Pharaoh and the plagues reminds us continually of our mortal, spiritual battle.

This contest is made even more compelling when we see that the plagues were directed against the gods of Egypt: "I will bring judgment on all the gods of Egypt. I am the LORD" (Ex. 12:12). All the gods were related to nature and many of them linked to the Nile. "The nearest thing to a truly national religion was the cult of Osiris and his cycle. . . . Osiris . . . [was] a god of vegetation link[ed] with the annual rise of the Nile and consequent rebirth of life."[1] The first nine plagues seem to have arisen out of the Nile, which was literally the source of Egypt's life. Twice a year it flooded, providing fertilization and adding to the available land through its delta soil deposits. It also provided the water supply for Egypt. Hymns were written for the blessing of the Nile. There is a document which likely was from a period close to the days described in Exodus:

> Hail to thee, Oh Nile, that issues from the earth and comes to keep Egypt alive! . . . He that waters the meadows which recreated in order to keep every kid alive. He that makes to drink the desert and the place distant from water: that is the dew coming down from heaven.[2]

By bringing plagues up out of the Nile God demonstrated that the gods of the Egyptians were impotent: they could not deliver what was claimed for them. Their presumed power and majesty were unmasked to demonstrate their bankruptcy. The reigning king is also exposed as irresponsible, unreliable and filled with duplicity.

So the ten plagues were unleashed as God's judgment and a mocking of the gods of Egypt. Scholars have suggested that all except the last plague arose, directly or indirectly, from the Nile. The pollution of the Nile may have caused frogs to seek unsuccessfully for clear water;

without it they died. This in turn could have produced lice, flies and disease to livestock and humans. Even plagues seven through nine may have been traced to the Nile: hail, little known in that part of the world, may have been caused by evaporation from the river; and locusts have been known to swarm to already-devastated fields and crops. The darkness may have been caused by massive duststorms that could be the culmination of such a set of catgastrophes.

THE TEN PLAGUES

1. Turning of water to blood	Exodus 7:19-25
2. Frogs	Exodus 8:1-15
3. Lice	Exodus 8:16-19
4. Flies	Exodus 8:20-32
5. Livestock disease	Exodus 9:1-7
6. Boils	Exodus 9:8-12
7. Hail	Exodus 9:13-35
8. Locusts	Exodus 10:1-20
9. Darkness	Exodus 10:21-29
10. Death of firstborn	Exodus 12:29, 30

It is especially exciting to see the story develop to a predetermined end. The end was predicted — "[H]e will not listen to you" (7:4)—and confirmed at the conclusion: "But the LORD hardened Pharaoh's heart, and he was not willing to let them go" (10:27). Yet there is a pointed development in the attitude of Pharaoh. In the first two plagues the magicians matched the miracles of Moses and Aaron as they turned the water to blood and brought frogs in the land. In the third plague the magicians failed and confessed their defeat, saying to Pharaoh, "This is the finger of God" (8:19). The magicians did not try again on the fourth (flies), fifth (livestock disease) or sixth (boils on men and animals): they themselves suffered from the boils. The judgment is turned on them and they disappear from the narrative.

Pharaoh is the stubborn tyrant to the bitter end. As the frogs overwhelm him he appeals to Moses and Aaron, even promising release. But when the frogs are dead he changes his mind. In the plague of lice he is simply defiant. In the fourth plague he offers a compromise — they can worship, but only in Egypt. When Moses refuses, Pharaoh allows for a wilderness feast as close as possible to Egypt. But again, when the plague of flies ends, he withdraws his permission. His defiance expresses itself again in the fifth and sixth plagues. The hail forces Pharaoh to confess his sin and grant their release. As the plague ends, his stubbornness returns. Something new emerges in the eighth plague when Pharaoh's servants beg him to relent for the sake of the nation, and he consents to let only the menfolk go. Again Moses refuses, the locusts come and devour the crops, and Pharaoh confesses and prays for the fourth time that the plague will be removed. This time he offers no concessions. As the locusts are removed he maintains his refusal. With the ninth plague, darkness, he finally makes his greatest concession. All Israel can go, but flocks and herds must stay as security for the people's return. Again Moses refuses and the dialogue ends.

A progression is also seen in the first five plagues when Pharaoh hardened his heart (7:22; 8:15, 19, 32; 9:7). After the fifth plague *the Lord* hardened Pharaoh's heart (9:12; 10:20, 27; 11:10). So Yahweh turned the Egyptians' gods against them as the source of their judgment. The Nile that was supposed to bring life and health brought devastation. The plagues are also a litany to the stubbornness of Pharaoh, who was like the ninepin in the narrative — set up to be knocked down, and knocked down to be set up again. God makes a fool out of Pharaoh: "The kings of the earth take their stand and the rulers gather together against the LORD . . . . The One enthroned in heaven laughs; the Lord scoffs at them" (Ps. 2:2, 4).

The God who humbled Pharaoh and his gods rules the world today. The nations will rage in rebellion against God with their Hitlers, Mussolinis and Latin American generals; but God is sovereign in the affairs of men. In the church we need not cower at the humanistic forces but take our bold stand for Jesus Christ. The plagues testify that God is all-powerful and willing to deliver. He performs what he has promised. A bold stand must be taken by the people of God on the moral issues of the day. There may often be times when Christians must say to those in authority, "We must obey God rather than men." That will be especially true when the people of God are not permitted freely to worship and serve the Lord.

God's Grace to Israel

Have you ever wondered why the Israelites were unaffected by the plagues? After all, as we have noted, they were associated with the idolatry of Egypt. The sovereign grace of God alone accounts for this distinction. The Pentateuch repeatedly makes it plain that Israel's privilege rested upon the free, sovereign grace of God (Deut. 7:7; 9:4-6). The effect of God's grace on the life of Israel is clearly stated: "[O]n that day I will deal differently with the land of Goshen, where my people live; no swarms of flies will be there" (Ex. 8:22). Another possible translation of that verse is, "I will put division [or set redemption] between my people and Egypt." Israel was in the process of being redeemed. God's blessing rested on them while he punished Egypt. These acts of God were, by his grace, the "loving reacquisition of something formerly possessed."[3] God was reasserting his ownership of Israel.

Furthermore, by great signs and wonders God showed his power over Satan and evil. For this reason the plagues can be compared to the miracles of Jesus. In the exodus the question arose, Would the power of Egypt prevail over the promises of God? In Jesus' day the question was, Would the power of Rome and Jewry prevail over God's Son? In both instances the miracles mark the triumph of Christ over Satan: "The reason the Son of God appeared was to destroy the devil's work" (1 John 3:8).

Our individual lives, families and churches are surrounded by the world. Nothing in this world can deliver us from sin and its bondage. God alone saves us by his omnipotent power. Furthermore, in this conflict we as believers have his promised victory. But we are warned that the conflict will involve "a strong man, fully armed" (Luke 11:21) and thus will demand total commitment and a counting of the cost of such warfare (Luke 14:31). Since we fight "against the rulers, against the authorities, against the powers of this dark world and against the spiritual forces of evil in the heavenly realms" (Eph. 6:12), our weapons are not of this world but are spiritual weapons. In this battle we are promised a victory by the Lord that is shared by his people. The plagues that bring victory over Pharaoh and his gods point to ultimate victory in Christ: "Having disarmed the powers and authorities, he made a public spectacle of them, triumphing over them by the cross" (Col. 2:15).

Notes

1. K. A. Kitchen, "Egypt," *New Bible Dictionary* (Grand Rapids: Eerdmans Press, 1962), 351.

2. Quoted by John J. Davies in *Moses and Gods of Egypt* (Grand Rapids: Baker Book House, 1971), 91.

3. Geerhardus Vos, *Biblical Theology* (Grand Rapids: Eerdmans Press, 1948), 129.

Review Questions

1. What does the Hebrew word for "plague" mean? What twofold purpose of God does it describe?

2. What progression takes place in the story of the plagues?

3. How can the plagues be compared to the miracles of Jesus?

Discussion Questions

1. Discuss the ways in which salvation and judgment are linked in Scripture.

2. Read Revelation 4. How does it reiterate the exodus-plague motif?

3. How should the victory over Pharaoh affect the Christian life?

8

THE RESURRECTION OF ISRAEL

We live in a death-denying culture. We seek to restrain death's coming by medical and psychological means. When it does come we either trivialize it or succumb to despair. Death also obsessed the Egyptian people. The real power of their priesthood lay in their promise to guarantee a safe passage to the future world under the rule of Osiris, the god of vegetation. Since the body was attached to the soul, mummification became the means of preserving the two together. Earthly possessions filled an Egyptian's tomb because this was the eternal dwelling place. The Passover message of hope and resurrection contrasts with the despair of the Egyptians and of modern man.

We have noted several times how the pattern of God's revelation consists of promise and fulfillment (word and act). We see this pattern continuing as Moses brackets the Passover event with a preceding and succeeding interpretation.

Exodus 11:1-9	God's word of promise and explanation
Exodus 12:1-20	Instructions for passover
Exodus 12:21-28	Orders transmitted to the people
Exodus 12:29-42	Actual events of the Passover
Exodus 12:43-49	Passover participation defined
Exodus 12:50, 51	The exodus accomplished
Exodus 13:1-16	Interpretation of the promise and fulfillment, and their application

The Last Plague

In Exodus 11-13 there is not a strict chronology of events. The organization of the material in much of the Old Testament had a different purpose. Moses was describing a historical event not as a scientific recital of historical fact but as a redemptive revelation with moral implications. Here the chronology of events might have been:

The plague of darkness (Ex. 10:21-23);

During the darkness, instruction for the final plagues (11:1-3) and the Passover (12:1-28);

Moses' confrontation with Pharaoh and his hardening (10:24-29);

The conclusion of the confrontation and Moses' departure (11:4-8);

Moses' summary of the plagues (11:9, 10);

The plague on the firstborn (12:29, 30);

The exodus (12:31-42).

The Lord told the Israelites to prepare to leave, because one more plague was coming. With that plague God would deliver his people. The Israelites asked their neighbors for jewels, silver and gold. Were the people of God begging or even borrowing? Certainly after years of slavery the Egyptians owed much to Israel, but it was God who put it into the hearts of the Egyptians to give these things. Though Pharaoh was hard-hearted, the people were terrified at the power of Yahweh and sought by any means to placate him. Further, in those days when an army was victorious it received the spoils of its enemy as a symbol of victory.

Now Moses describes the nature of the last plague. At midnight Yahweh would pass through the land of Egypt and bring death to the firstborn of both man and animals. Why the firstborn? They were considered the heirs of all the rights of property and position. The death of the firstborn reveals that God's redemption involves a judgment on sin and evil. The holiness of God requires that he hate sin. The violent destruction of Sodom and Gomorrah (Gen. 18, 19) represented a supernatural judgment of God. From the entrance of evil into the world God's judgment on sin was death: "[F]or when you eat of it [the tree of the knowledge of good and evil] you will surely die" (Gen. 2:17). God's judgment comes on Egypt not only because of their general guilt but also for their disobeying of his command to let his firstborn, Israel, go (Ex. 4:22, 23). By this means Pharaoh would know the distinction between Israelites and Egyptians, because not even a dog would bark in Israel in contrast to the loud wailing of the Egyptians.

In our Christian circles we often shrink from the idea of God's judgment. To do that is to shrink from an acknowledgment of the nature of God. His justice and holiness demand that he be a God who deals with sin. Furthermore, a gospel message that leaves out the message of sin's consequence is a false gospel. We need to praise God for his justice just as much as for his love. In our witnessing we must communicate that sin deserves judgment. "[M]an is destined to die once, and after that to face judgment" (Heb. 9:27). The good news is that Christ delivers us from our deserved judgment. God had been patient and had given ample warning to the Egyptians, but they had turned hard hearts to the warning of God. Now there must be judgment.

The apostle Paul's comment is appropriate here: "So when you, a mere man, pass judgment on them and yet do the same things, do you think you will escape God's judgment? Or do you show contempt for the riches of his kindness, tolerance and patience, not realizing that God's kindness leads you toward repentance? But because of your stubbornness and your unrepentant heart, you are storing up wrath against yourself for the day of God's wrath, when his righteous judgment will be revealed. God 'will give to each person according to what he has done.' . . . For God does not show favoritism" (Rom. 2:3-6, 11).

Moses as God's representative reflected God's justice. He left Pharaoh "hot with anger" (Ex. 11:8). We need something of that anger toward evil. This must never be expressed toward an individual, because we are called to love our enemies. But it must be felt and expressed toward the systems and religious philosophies, the "rulers and authorities" of the satanic kingdom. When we pray "[Y]our kingdom come . . . on earth as it is in heaven" we are praying, among other things, that the kingdom of Satan would be destroyed. Since Moses is the Old Testament redeemer, his anger directly expresses the Lord's anger. Should not our prayers reflect some of this anger toward sin? Shouldn't our protests of social and political oppression possess an edge of anger? Consider, for example, those nations where our brothers and sisters in Christ are not free to worship or evangelize. That should fill us with godly anger as we pray for their freedom.

Nothing destroys a Christian's prayer life more than resignation to the *status quo*. For example, we may be indifferent to secularism, which sees life as an end in itself. We find it easy to come to terms with an unjust and fallen world even when it intrudes into our churches. We have lost our anger in prayer. We must be genuinely angry that God's name is hallowed so little, his kingdom comes so feebly and his will is done so seldom. God has not lost his wrath and neither should we lose ours! Moses is a model of anger, not only in his dealings with Pharaoh but also in prayer to God.

The Passover

The yearly timing of the Passover gives us further insight into its symbolism and significance for God's people. The way nations and cultures mark their months and years often reveals something about their religion. The events described in Exodus 12 mark a very important time in Israel's history when the children of Israel began to divide the year into months. From the standpoint of a religious calendar, the Passover and the exodus would begin the first month. So the new year for Israel is now grounded not in nature-renewal but in a redemptive-historical event —the Passover and exodus. The Egyptian new year began with the onset of the flood of the Nile. In structuring their calendars all the ancient cultures followed nature or lunar movement, but not Israel: "Such a revolutionary phenomenon is without analogy in the ancient world."[1] God's redemptive act would commence the Israelite new year. At the center of Israel's life as a nation would stand the remembrance of God's redemption.

In seeking to understand and apply Exodus 12 we must distinguish between what the Lord instructed for the eve of the exodus (the slaughtering, the eating in haste and the application of blood to the doorposts, vss 1-13) and what Israel was to do each year in the celebration of the day (the Passover and Feast of Unleavened Bread, vss 14-20).

Israel was God's firstborn, chosen in Abraham. Nevertheless the Israelites deserved God's judgment because they too were sinners. How would they be spared this judgment on the firstborn? If they were to be saved from judgment they must obey God by providing a lamb and sprinkling its blood on their lintels and doorposts. God would provide redemption through the slaying of a lamb. On the fourteenth day of the month every Israelite family brought a lamb to their home and killed it. To meet the requirements of God the lamb had to be a male, one year old and without defect. After the animal was slain the blood was sprinkled on the doorposts of the house (see 12:22), thus representing the protection of the house.

Verse 22 describes the manner of application with hyssop. The door symbolized not only entrance but the place of security. The lamb was the substitute appointed by God and slain in place of the son. This great act of the Passover shows that salvation is never *earned* by sinful humans. God loved Israel and would keep his promises to Abraham, and thus they were spared. They too deserved the visit of the death angel, for they were no better than Egypt. Here God demonstrates the fact that salvation comes only by his grace.

The Passover is a picture of redemption in Jesus Christ. John the Baptist said of Jesus, "Look, the Lamb of God, who takes away the sin of the world!" (John 1:29). John pointed to Jesus as the fulfillment of the Passover lamb and the one who could actually take away the sins of his people. The sacrificial Passover lamb could only *point* to redemption and cleansing: Christ alone could actually take away sin. The sprinkling of blood eloquently speaks of a substituting atonement. The lamb was the substitute for the firstborn, thus bearing the penalty of death in place of the one offering the sacrifice. So Jesus Christ, the Lamb of God, suffers and dies in the place of guilty sinners (1 Pet. 1:2, Rom. 5:8, 9, Heb. 9:13, 14). By his grace God chose us to be his firstborn son and sent his Son to suffer and die to remove sin and its penalty, death.

The Feast of Unleavened Bread

Such a dramatic deliverance would make an indelible impression on all of Israel, especially a firstborn son. He had been spared by the blood of the lamb. So the Passover and the Feast of Unleavened Bread were established as memorials to commemorate this special redemption. The Feast of Unleavened Bread lasted for seven days during which the Israelites ate bread without leaven. Leaven causes the bread to rise and gives it sweetness, but here it designates evil (Lev. 2:11, 1 Cor. 5:7, 8). All the leaven was to be put out of the house. On the first day of the feast a convocation was held and, as on a sabbath, no work was to be done on that day. The celebration of the feast concluded with public worship throughout the nation. Both the Passover and the Feast of Unleavened Bread were to be celebrated forever.

Once Moses had received the full instructions about the Passover and the Feast of Unleavened Bread he declared them to the elders and the people (Ex. 12:21-28). As a practical man Moses told the Israelites how to apply the blood using a brush made from hyssop. Washing and cleansing commanded by later Levitical law was often effected by hyssop (Lev. 14:4, Ps. 51:7, Heb. 9:19). The pungent smells from the spilt blood and the roasting meat necessitated the strongly aromatic covering from the hyssop.

Passover meant a feast of communion with the Lord. You can hear the children asking, "Why the hyssop? Why the lamb?" Passover became one of the three great festivals of Israel and a powerful aid to the preservation and proclamation of this great redemptive event. The Passover ritual was followed by the seven-day Feast of Unleavened Bread. The two events combined as a celebration and memorial of the exodus, and the Israelites' descendants would be guaranteed participation in the events of the exodus. By eating the bread of affliction (Ex. 12:3-10) they, in a measure, shared the personal experience of their ancestors.

The New Testament uses the Passover and Feast of Unleavened Bread as major symbols. At the Last Supper Jesus ate a Passover meal with his disciples. John records that the procedure in Roman law of breaking a victim's bones was waived so that Jesus could exemplify the Passover lamb (John 19:36). Paul adopts the Passover feast as a Christian festal celebration: "Your boasting is not good. Don't you know that a little yeast works through the whole batch of dough? Get rid of the old yeast that you may be a new batch without yeast — as you really are. For Christ, our Passover lamb, has been sacrificed. Therefore let us keep the Festival, not with the old yeast, the yeast of malice and wickedness, but with bread without yeast, the bread of sincerity and truth" (1 Cor. 5:6-8). The *Lamb of God* title appears twenty-seven times as the symbol for Jesus in the book of Revelation.

Paul affirms that Jesus Christ is the true Passover (deliverer from sin); through him believers have become a new bread without leaven. Leavened bread is used negatively to mean malice and evil. The New Testament feast of the Lord's Supper reminds us of our redemption and the price that was paid. But it also forces us to see our calling, as the New Israel, to leave Egypt and the leaven of the old sinful life. Evil lurks at the door of our hearts in the form of bad attitudes and lusts. In our relationship with our neighbors malice and hatred often spring up in our hearts, especially toward those who, by scorn or by just ignoring us, mock our Christian faith. Sometimes non-Christian neighbors will not speak to us because of our testimony for Christ, and we can harbor hatred toward them in our hearts. The New Testament feast says, as does the Old, Don't go back to the leaven of Egypt; rather remember your deliverance in Christ and thus live lives of sincerity and truth.

Death and Deliverance

At the appointed midnight hour the Lord fulfilled his promise by bringing the judgment of God upon all the firstborn of Egypt. This judgment knew no respect of persons, and the firstborn of Pharaoh was slain as well as the son of the poorest in the land. This dreadful event awakened Pharaoh and his servants, for it was not a silent and painless death. Egypt rang with the grief of every family. Escape from the previous plagues might have been rationalized, but this one Pharaoh could not escape. Pharaoh saw the son he loved and cherished, his successor to the throne, now lying on his bed lifeless and limp. The heart and spirit of Pharaoh changed, and he simply let the children of Israel go. No qualifications now, no concessions; in fact, the leaving was on Moses' terms (Ex. 12:32). So powerful were these events that a mixed multitude went with Israel out of Egypt. Many Egyptians had followed Israel's example and sacrificed a lamb and had received shelter under the blood. Once identified with Israel, they had to obey the ordinances in order to remain Israelites and come within the family of Israel. They also had to be circumcised to be part of the perpetual feasts of Passover and Unleavened Bread (12:49).

The whole account ends with the simple but dramatic statement: "The LORD brought the Israelites out of Egypt by their divisions" (12:51). Slaves under the sentence of death were freed to a new life by the lamb of God.

Everyone reading these words, if the Lord tarries long enough in his coming, will die. The Bible describes death as our enemy (1 Cor. 15). It further proclaims that death is not just a natural enemy but the result of our sinfulness (Gen. 2:17). Death comes as the just sentence on our sin and refers, in the Bible, to our spiritual separation from God (Eph. 2:1), physical death (1 Cor. 15) and eternal separation from God (Heb. 9:27). The relevance and power of the gospel are clear when we face the stark reality of death. The Lamb of God slain for the sins of his people is the only source of life in the midst of death.

Our celebration of the Lord's Supper, the New Testament Passover, must always be with the realization that we deserve death. The people of God are inexcusable sinners and righteously condemned criminals, but by the grace of God Jesus has suffered death for us. The power, beauty and glory of God's grace can be fully learned and experienced only in the context of this biblical truth.

Note

1. Nahum M. Sarna, *Exploring Exodus* (New York: Schocken Books, 1986), 85.

Review Questions

1. What is the significance of the judgment on the firstborn?
2. How do we resemble Israel's firstborn?
3. What events commemorated the exodus? What event commemorates our redemption?

Discussion Questions

1. What should be our attitude toward judgment? toward anger?
2. How can your study of the exodus better enable you to prepare for the Lord's Supper?
3. How does reflecting on death bring out the reality of the gospel?

9

THE SONG OF TRIUMPH AT THE SEA

The great deliverance had come. Pharaoh summoned Moses in the middle of the night and ordered Israel to leave the country. The Egyptians went to their neighbors and pleaded with them to leave. And the Israelites did leave even before their preparations were complete, loaded down with dough for bread and presents of gold, silver and precious stones from the Egyptians.

The Israelite son who had been spared by the blood of the lamb was now called to go forth to a new life with the people of God. Since their lives had been spared it was appropriate that they be consecrated (Ex. 13:1, 2, 11-16). This consecration applied not only to male children but to animals as well. Even the unclean animals (that is, those that did not part the hoof — see Lev. 11:1-8) were given a means of being set apart. The donkey was probably selected as a representative for unclean beasts that were to be set apart. Both firstborn human beings and animals had benefited from the redemption and thus should be dedicated (set apart to the Lord).

Think how the firstborn son in an Israelite home must have felt. A terrible judgment had come and he could hear the country's cries of sorrow. Perhaps he had held the bowl while his father sprinkled the blood on doorposts and lintel. To have been saved by the blood of the lamb would remain a moving affirmation, and now this dedication was a concrete application of that redemption to his life. Far too often consecration is thought of in negative terms, but it involves both separation *from* the world and separation *to* God.

Our calling in Christ also demands consecration. Negatively, we must regularly deal with sin in all of its expression: every day we must take our sins of lust, greed and hatred and leave them at the cross. We frequently fail to own up to sin and its consequences. But the wailing of the Egyptians as they experienced God's judgment riveted his hatred for sin upon the minds of the firstborn of Israel so that they would be moved to give themselves to God.

Positively, consecration means a total dedication to the Lord. Many of our material blessings, such as cars or vacations, stand in the way of a whole-souled dedication to God. We must receive these gifts with open hand, ready at any time to give them up when they hinder our dedication to Christ. In view of the great redemption wrought by the blood of the Lamb of God, Jesus Christ, Paul says, "Therefore, I urge you, brothers, in view of God's mercy, to offer your bodies as living sacrifices, holy and pleasing to God — which is your spiritual act of worship" (Rom. 12:1). If we have a vivid memory of God's mercy in his work of redemption, we will be moved to take our hands off our lives and consecrate them to Christ.

God Leads His People

A mixed crowd who wished to worship the Lord for his grace and mighty deeds left Egypt. As they began their exodus they remembered one promise made long ago.

Joseph, Jacob's son who had been prime minister of Egypt, had carefully taken his father's body back to Canaan. As his own death neared he too had made the Israelites swear that they would take *his* bones back to the promised land (Gen. 50:24, 25). In faith Joseph had been looking forward to the time when the children of Israel would return to the land of promise. As they left Egypt that night they carried with them a unique cargo, the mummified body of Joseph.

As one can see on the map below, the obvious way to Canaan is along the sea coast into Palestine. Why did the Lord lead the people in a circuitous route? The answer is that the sea route would have brought the people into direct battle with the Philistines. The children of Israel had to be trained to trust their Lord. Though they had seen his great wonders, their faith would soon falter. God took them instead by the way of the Sinai peninsula to Canaan.

Meanwhile God guided the children of Israel by a great cloud. It went before the people as a pillar of cloud by day and a pillar of fire at night. In the ancient world signal fires and smoke often led the people. But for Israel God himself was the signal fire.

God sovereignly appeared to Israel in the cloud. Theological study of this biblical phenomenon reveals the significance of God's showing his presence in the cloud as the King of glory. The cloud symbolized the personal presence of God and his sovereign power. By means of the cloud God moved on a mission of surveillance and judgment. Soon the voice of God would come from the midst of the cloud at Sinai, even as he spoke centuries later on the Mount of Transfiguration (Mark 9). Throughout the

Bible God leads, speaks and reveals by cloud and fire. We read many beautiful references to the cloud in the rest of the Old Testament. By night it lighted their path in glory; by day it shielded them from heat (Is. 4:5, 6).

From Etham the Lord led his people in a strange way, for he turned them back and sent them south to a place where they were hemmed in on either side. Before them was the Red Sea. It was called the "Reed" Sea and we are unsure of its location, but we are certain that it was a spot where they were surrounded by sea and wilderness. The Lord told Moses that he was again prepared to demonstrate his power over Pharaoh, who thought the slaves were confused and had lost their way. Overwhelmed by sorrow and regretting his mistake in letting Israel go, Pharaoh set out to bring the slaves back to Egypt.

Can you picture the chariots racing out against Israel? Six hundred of them roaring across the desert, open vehicles encircled by a two-foot rim with a footboard at the rear. These were fearsome military weapons. A charioteer and a warrior occupied each chariot, one free to drive, the other to drive his lance or sword through the enemy. Imagine the fearful word that spread through the Israelite camp: "They are coming with all their chariots!" (Ex. 14:10).

However, their cries soon turned into a bitter complaint against Moses, their words taking the form of sarcasm and irony. The Israelites displayed their incredibly short memory when they cried, "It would have been better for us to serve the Egyptians than to die in the desert!" (14:12). Their reaction is typical of the people of God when their spiritual perspectives are conditioned by circumstances. Shallow responses to the trauma of the moment are the

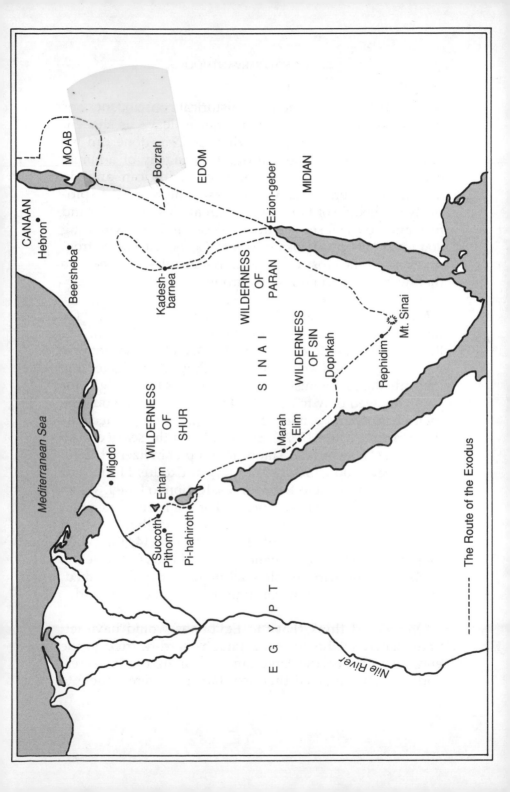

Mediterranean Sea

CANAAN
Hebron
Beersheba

MOAB

Bozrah

EDOM

Ezion-geber

MIDIAN

Kadesh-barnea

WILDERNESS
OF
PARAN

S I N A I

WILDERNESS
OF SIN

Dophkah

Mt. Sinai

Rephidim

WILDERNESS
OF
SHUR

Migdol

Etham

Succoth
Pithom

Pi-hahiroth

Marah
Elim

E G Y P T

Nile River

- - - - - - - - The Route of the Exodus

bane of believers. Without an historical consciousness of what God can do, many circumstances leave us shaken. Only by a consciousness of what God *has* done can we have faith in what God *will* do. The tragedy of a family death or seemingly insurmountable odds can and do frighten believers. Satanic enemies come to defeat spiritually the people of God. But the great message is, "Stand firm and you will see the deliverance the LORD will bring you today" (14:13). Looking back to God's deliverance from sin through the cross of Jesus Christ enables us to believe that he can and will bring us through our difficult times.

Moses gave the Israelites three commands: first, "Do not be afraid"; second, "Stand firm"; third, "[S]ee the deliverance [of] the LORD" (14:13). The Israelites did not prepare their swords and chariots — they didn't have any. Instead Moses promised them, "The LORD will fight for you; you need only to be still" (14:14). The Lord would be their chariots and armies. Moses' staff accomplished this deliverance (14:16; 4:17, 20). Stretched over the sea, it caused it to part. (The word *staff* stands for scepter in Ezekiel 12:10, 13 and Revelation 2:27; 12:5; 19:15.) In Exodus 14 the staff served as judgment to Egypt and salvation to Israel. When the Egyptians drew near, the angel of the Lord in the pillar of cloud went to the rear of the camp so that he stood between the Israelites and the Egyptians (14:20). When Moses stretched out his hand the Lord caused the sea to divide and the wind to blow all night to dry the seabed. Then the Lord led them through the sea on dry ground.

One would think that the Egyptians would have left immediately for home; but Pharaoh, hard-hearted to the end, commanded the Egyptians to pursue the Israelites, and the Lord afflicted them so that they were unable to pursue the fleeing multitude (cf Ps. 77:18, 19). They turned in panic and cried, "Let's get away from the Israelites! The LORD is fighting for them against Egypt" (14:25). But it was too late. On the opposite shore Moses lifted his staff, and the waters covered the host of Pharaoh in the midst of the sea. In sharp contrast to their unbelief and rebellion against Moses, we read of the people's reaction: "And when the Israelites saw the great power the LORD displayed against the Egyptians, the people feared the LORD and put their trust in him and in Moses his servant" (Ex. 14:31).

This crossing of the Red Sea became a cardinal affirmation of Old Testament faith. The Israelite people rehearsed it again and again. It was not only their salvation but also the judgment of God on Egypt. Israel left Egypt as fleeing slaves but emerged as a people who belonged to God and had experienced his deliverance. Isaiah joined this great biblical event to the creation of the world, for in both creation and exodus God worked the impossible. The church in the midst of impossible odds serves the God of creation and exodus: "Was it not you who dried up the sea, the waters of the great deep, who made a road in the depths of the sea so that the redeemed might cross over?" (Is. 51:10). The exodus is affirmed in the historical books (Judg. 6:8, 9, 13, 1 Sam. 12:6, 8, 1 Kings 8:51), celebrated in the psalms (78:13; 114:1, 3; 106:7-11) and given preaching force in the prophets (Hos. 11:1; Jer. 7:21; 11:1; Is. 10:24, 26).

The stunning victory of Yahwah over the Egyptians and the resultant jubilation evoked response in song. The Israelites watched the bodies of Egyptians float to the shore and realized, "That could have been me!" Thus they broke into a paean of victory. The song itself gives us a significant interpretation of the event, for it praises God as the sole agent of salvation. Israel did not cooperate or even lift a finger; even Moses' work is omitted. Yahwah alone effected the miracle.

The song does not contain new revelation about God, but it praises that climactic moment when Yahweh demonstrated himself as the Sovereign LORD of the flood, the winds, the host of Pharaoh and the redeemed Israelites. Not only does Israel's praise apply to the exodus experience, it also extends far into the future. Moses' song functions as a song of remembrance and also as an encouragement for the years ahead. "In your unfailing love you will lead the people you have redeemed. In your strength you will guide them . . . . [A]nguish will grip the people of Philistia. The chiefs of Edom will be terrified" (Ex. 15:13-15). Encouraged by victory at the Red Sea, they should press on to the promised land and triumph over Edom, Philistia and others. Thus Moses moves back and forth throughout the song from past to present to future. This pattern is a feature of God's praise as the God who makes a promise, keeps it, and therefore will continue to be faithful. This is precisely the pattern we have noted previously — a word of promise and an act of fulfillment. Here that pattern becomes the subject of God-honoring praise.

Therefore Moses' song became a pattern for the praise of God's people. We can find this pattern in the psalms.

Moses' Song: Exodus 15	*Psalms*
Yahweh is praised for his greatness and power (vs 6) and these are joined to his holiness (vs 13).	⟶ Psalm 89:14, 15

He displays his deeds of redemption and incomparable majesty (vs 11). ⟶ Psalm 77:14; 95:3

His display of omnipotence is to create a people for himself (vs 13). ⟶ Psalm 77:16

This display is before the nations (vs 14). ⟶ Psalm 98:2

The nations' gods are worthless before Yahweh (vs 14). ⟶ Psalm 96:5

He rules the world from his throne (vs 18). ⟶ Psalm 93:1ff; 96:7ff

This song has in view not only an immediate victory but the anticipation of a future victory over all of Canaan. The praise of this song is not just by a single person, Moses, but by all of Israel, and was sung and rehearsed at the sanctuary where "The LORD will reign for ever and ever" (15:1-18). Praise to God can be enhanced by careful study of this song. The first part of the song recounts Yahweh's victory at the sea. Strength and boldness characterize the meter, yet the thoughts are simple truth. Two features dominate the praise.

First, Yahweh is praised for his greatness and power (15:3, 6, 7, 11, 12, 16). The metaphor and anthropomorphic language vividly enliven the song. Meditate on this language and let its beauty and power stir your soul:

> The LORD is a warrior (vs 3);
> Your right hand, O LORD, was majestic in power (vs 6);
> You unleashed your burning anger (vs 7);
> The blast of your nostrils (vs 8);

I will draw my sword and my hand will destroy them
(vs 9);
[Y]ou blew with your breath, and the sea covered
them (vs 10).

Second, the specific and concrete elements of the victory
are recounted. The victory song turns from the historical
event to the praise of God, and it focuses on the shattering
defeat inflicted on the proud Egyptians. The high-and-
mighty armies of Pharaoh sank ignominiously into the
sea. "Your right hand, O LORD, was majestic in power"
(15:16).

The second part of this victory song begins in verse 13.
Now the song interprets the event in relationship to Israel,
with no further reference to victory at the sea. The redemption of Israel from Egypt leads eventually to the possession of the promised land. The Abrahamic promise
appears again. Israel has become a nation, and now God
will bring them to their land. He not only redeems a people
for himself but also brings them to the land. Furthermore
the song ends with Israel's role in the land as a worshiping
servant people, singing on Mount Zion in God's sanctuary.

There is a striking parallel between the first part of the
song and the second:

First Part	Second Part
Danger from Egyptians vss 1, 2	Threats of nations vss 13-15
Like a stone (sure victory) vs 5	Like a stone (sure victory) vs 16
Majesty of God vs 6	Majestic in holiness, awesome in glory vs 11

102

Thus even the song's structure seems to reflect the pattern of praise for the events at the Red Sea and encouragement for the future victory of Israel.

The hymn recounts the redemptive history from the exodus to the securing of Zion, because the exodus is the fulfillment of God's promise to make from Abraham's seed a nation and to bring them to the land. The people of God respond to him in praise because of his covenant faithfulness in keeping his promise. Much of the singing might have taken the form of one group responding to another. Miriam's exhortation, "Sing to the LORD" (15:20), is responded to by the women of Israel. Thus Israel's exodus from Egypt ends with exultant praise; even the women sang and danced and made music.

Israel's Song and Our Song

Turn now to Revelation 15:3. Here we find the song that we will sing at the last great triumph of the people of God, the song of Moses and the Lamb sung by all God's people at the consummation of Christ's kingdom. The great deliverance of Israel from the Egyptians pictures the deliverance of God's people in all ages from sin and death. The Israelites standing and singing at the Red Sea are a prophecy concerning those who will be victorious over Satan and will sing in the age of fulfillment the song of Moses and the Lamb. For us the song will resound with all the meaning and power of Calvary and with the victories over Satan granted to Christ's people.

Often our modern praise is individualistic. It is dominated by the personal pronouns *I* and *me*. It is related simply to the church today rather than to the church of all the ages. But praises that are sung should include a sense that we are joining with the angels and the hosts of heaven to praise our redeeming God.

All too often our churches are joyless. The recounting and remembrance of the grace of God discovered at Calvary and worked out in our lives should bring joy and praise not only to our hearts but also to our lips. The rather staid, solemn nature of our worship should be joined by times of ecstatic joy. Think of the women dancing and playing their tambourines. Most of us think that only the holy rollers do that, yet the Psalms are filled with clapping, dancing, shouting and joyous singing. However, no syrupy pietism is found in this song. It is objective, God-centered praise filled with God's justice and wrath as well as his love. Almost all of it is directed to the nature of God and his works.

While our modern praise is often personalistic and emotional, the Bible teaches us to praise God *as God* and to revel in his glory. Our consuming passion should be to know and praise him in the fullness of his glory:

Sing to the LORD, for he is highly exalted (Ex. 15:20).

Review Questions

1. What does "consecration" mean? What did it mean for the Israelites? What does it mean for the Christian?

2. How did Israel fail to show "historical consciousness"?

3. Review some of the major features of Moses' song of victory. What past event does it celebrate? What future event does it anticipate?

Discussion Questions

1. How can you consecrate your life to Christ this week?

2. Compare your favorite hymns with the song of Moses. Are they self-centered or God-centered? Does your worship reflect the ecstatic joy of Moses? Is your approach to God filled with praise to the fullness of his glory?

10

FREE TO SERVE!

Bob Dylan's song says it so well: "You've got to serve somebody." Everyone directs his life toward some goal that can subordinate everything he does. When a man believes that his life can be fulfilled only by being president of the company, he gives his all to that end. He sacrifices family, personal relationships, everything for that goal. The woman who believes that marriage and family will give meaning to life will spend her days calculating how to find a husband. We have all seen people totally restructure their lives for a personal goal.

Everybody serves someone or something: it is part of our nature as human beings. But apart from Christ, Paul writes, we do not choose our master wisely: "They [mankind] exchanged the truth of God for a lie, and worshiped and served created things rather than the Creator" (Rom. 1:25). The question is not *whether* we will be servants but whom or what we will serve. The ways of life that serve the creature are as unlimited as the complexity of the creation and the imagination of the human heart. Some believe that accumulating wealth will bring fulfillment. Others opt for the simple life, advocating clean air and fighting pollution. Some pay to have their bodies frozen, hoping for a medical resurrection. Everybody pledges allegiance to some god and lives life in submission to it.

The redemptive work of Jesus Christ restores us to our proper servanthood by restoring us to our proper Master. Servanthood is at the heart of our calling as Christians. We have been *saved to serve*. We are to serve the Lord our God with all our heart, mind, soul and strength. Paul writes, "[O]ffer your bodies as living sacrifices, holy and pleasing to God — this is your spiritual act of worship [service]" (Rom. 12:1).

One of the major issues of the bondage in Egypt and the exodus was the freedom to serve. Note the chain of passages that stress this theme of redemption for service.

> *Exodus 4:22, 23* — Upon his return to Egypt Moses is to say to Pharaoh, "This is what the LORD says: . . . 'Let my son go, so he may worship [serve] me.' "

> *Exodus 7:16* — Before the first plague of blood in the Nile God has Moses warn Pharaoh, "Let my people go, so that they may worship [serve] me in the desert."

> *Exodus 8:1, 20; 9:1, 13; 10:3* — The constant demand during the plagues was basically the same: "Let my people go, so that they may worship [serve] me."

> *Exodus 10:8, 11* — When Pharaoh begins to relent, albeit often changing his mind or failing to meet the full demand, he shows that he understands the real issue, saying in effect, "Go, worship [serve] your God."

> *Exodus 12:31* — The climax of God's judgment on Pharaoh and Egypt results in Pharaoh's saying, "Up! Leave my people, you and the Israelites! Go, worship [serve] the LORD as you requested."

> *Exodus 14:12* — Ironically, the rebellion of Israel against the Lord and his servant Moses is expressed in similar terms: "Didn't we say to you in Egypt, 'Leave us

alone; let us serve the Egyptians'? It would have been better for us to serve the Egyptians than to die in the desert!"

You may have noticed that this writer has often added the word *serve* following *worship*. The Hebrew word translated "worship" in these passages actually means more than worship in the sense of sacrifices and praise or a gathering of believers for worship. The basic meaning of the word deals with our allegiance to a master in the totality of our lives. Moses preeminently reflected the meaning of the word when he wrote, "[T]he people feared the LORD and put their trust in him and in Moses his servant" (Ex. 14:31). The formal worship of the people of God simply expressed one dimension of that total service of life. So the word *worship* can refer to the general devotion and commitment of our lives as well as the formal acts of piety and corporate gathering which express that devotion.

A massive paradox now unfolds before us. Israel had been servants of Pharaoh, slaves in Egypt. Now by the blood of the lamb and the grace of God they have become slaves of Yahweh. This change in submission is a radical one: from Pharaoh, the enemy of God, to Moses, the friend of God. But our human hearts recoil from the idea that Israel is just a slave with a different master. Is God merely offering a change from one slavery to another? We have seen in Exodus 4 that Egypt is the symbol of sin and its consequent bondage, for "everyone who sins is a slave to sin" (John 8:34). But with Israel delivered from that bondage by the Passover and the parting of the sea, how are we to understand their new servanthood? In what way is it redeeming or renewing? One slavery changed to another cannot be freedom!

Sonship and Servanthood

Two aspects of Israel's new servanthood can help explain this paradox.

First, in the midst of the exodus God calls Israel not only his servants but also his sons. When God instructed Moses to go to Egypt to prepare for the exodus he said, "Then say to Pharaoh, 'This is what the LORD says: Israel is my firstborn son . . . [L]et my son go, so he may worship [serve] me' " (Ex. 4:22, 23). The words *son* or *daughter* have wrapped up in them all the sweetness and tenderness of the Father's love. When the angel of death seeks to come through the door, the Father God says No! because of the blood of the lamb. The firstborn were adopted into the family of God. That fatherly love is expressed in the protection of the glory cloud (the pillar of cloud by day and fire by night). So Israel is to be God's nation not with servile fear but with a joy and thankfulness that produce loving, willing obedience to their new master. The law given to Israel begins with a reminder of their relationship to God. "I am the LORD your God, who brought you out of Egypt, out of the land of slavery" (Ex. 20:2). The difference between slavery to God and bondage to Egypt lies in the fact that Israel served God as sons, not as despised slaves. The Ten Commandments and the other laws God gave his servants were given in the context of redemptive sonship.

Second, this new servanthood is simply a return to what God had intended human beings to be — his friends and servants. Genesis 1 and 2 describe beautifully the human calling to be God's servants: "Let us make man in our image . . . and let them rule over the fish of the sea and the birds of the air, over . . . livestock" (Gen. 1:28). The word *bless* means a face-to-face relationship. Adam and Eve were in the fullest sense son and daughter, friends and servants, of God. But sin devastated all of that. They became slaves to their own guilt, creatureliness, the serpent and death. Egypt was merely the outworking of that servile bondage to sin. God's redemption restores us to our original sonship and servanthood. Egypt was cruel and harsh because it was abnormal (contrary to creation order), but redemption restores us to what God intended at creation — willing, joyful service for God. We will see that Israel will fail in the wilderness, refuse their creational servanthood and turn back to the gods of Egypt. But for a moment, as we reflect on Exodus 13-15, we see that redemption is inherently a call to the servanthood of sons.

Israel's Adoption and Ours

The apostle Paul picks up this theme of Israel's adoption and privileges: "Theirs is the adoption as sons; theirs the divine glory" (Rom. 9:4). The adoption as sons clearly refers to Israel as the Lord's firstborn son. That dramatic theme of the Lord's loving, fatherly relation to Israel by his grace unfolds throughout the Old Testament (Deut. 14:1, 2; Is. 63:16; 64:8; Hos. 11:1). The glory referred to in Romans is the glory in the cloud of the Lord's presence as it protected them at the sea and especially as it appeared on Mount Sinai (Ex. 24:16, 17). The glory dwelling among them certified to Israel that God not only called them his sons but also dwelt with them and among them (Ex. 29:42-46).

Israel's adoption must be carefully distinguished from the adoption of sons described in the New Testament.

Paul in Galatians 4:4, 5 shows how the two are different: "But when the time had fully come, God sent his Son, born of a woman, born under law, to redeem those under law, that we might receive the full rights as sons." The people of Israel redeemed from Egypt were children of God, but they were children who were "underage." The old covenant that God made through Moses prepared for the new covenant made through Christ, and its fulfillment and consummation. Israel was immature, and their immaturity was connected to the incompleteness of Old Testament revelation and the fact that the Holy Spirit had not come in all his fullness. Israel needed the instruction they received from the ceremonies and theophanies (appearances of God). Because they had incomplete Bibles and Pentecost had not yet come, they needed the myriads of symbols and sacrifices.

But believers in the New Testament age have the full blessing of sonship without the discipline of the Mosaic era. "You are all sons of God through faith in Christ Jesus, for all of you who were baptized into Christ have clothed yourselves with Christ" (Gal. 3:26, 27). Israel was undoubtedly overwhelmed by the blessings of the Passover and the parting of the Red Sea, but the fulfillment of the redemption that we receive in Christ is the greatest privilege:

> The law is only a shadow of the good things that are coming—not the realities themselves. For this reason it can never, by the same sacrifices repeated endlessly year after year, make perfect those who draw near to worship. . . . By faith he [Moses] left Egypt, not fearing the king's anger; he persevered because he saw him who is invisible. By faith he kept the Passover and the sprinkling of blood, so that the destroyer of the firstborn would not touch the firstborn of Israel.

. . . These were all commended for their faith, yet
none of them received what had been promised. God
had planned something better for us so that only
together with us would they be made perfect (Heb.
10:1; 11:27, 28, 39, 40).

One of the most neglected benefits of our salvation in
Jesus Christ is adoption. The cry of our culture is for self-
esteem. In a provocative book entitled *The Culture of Narcissism* Christopher Lasch underscores our craze to find a
sense of self-worth: "The only reality is the identity [a
person] can construct out of materials furnished by adver-
tising and mass culture, themes of popular film and fic-
tion."[1] Jesse Jackson, a black religious leader, encourages
black children to chant, "I am somebody!" because much
of American culture has robbed black men and women of
a dignified view of self. The biblical notion of adoption is
our great affirmation over against the confused zeal of our
culture for self-esteem. As believers we do not have to
look in the mirror, or at the amount of money in our
pocketbook, for our dignity. When we turn from the slavery of sin to Jesus Christ we cry, "I am somebody—a child
of the King!" "To all who received him, to those who
believed in his name, he gave the right to become children
of God" (John 1:12).

But what is the purpose of this mighty deliverance from
bondage, this new relationship with God? His covenant
with Abraham involved a mission for the descendants of
Abraham: "I will make your name great, and you will be a
blessing. I will bless those who bless you, and whoever
curses you I will curse; and all peoples on earth will be
blessed through you" (Gen. 12:2, 3). The Bible defines the
servant as one who fulfills God's mission, which is directed
not only to Israel but also to the whole world. The children

of Israel were to be a servant nation bringing blessing to all nations. The New Testament teaches that, having been servants of sin, believers have a new status (Gal. 4:5, Rom. 8:15, 23), free from enslavement to sin, and by the grace of God now free to serve the Lord. When Christ saves his people they become his own possession. They have new direction and goals that shape their lives. Paul says, "You, my brothers, were called to be free. But do not use your freedom to indulge the sinful nature; rather, serve one another in love" (Gal. 5:13).

As we have seen, the Old Testament uses the word *serve* for the call to commitment, obedience and mission, and for worship. It is in worship that dependence and service find their climax. The ceremonial acts of worship were intended to remind Israel of their utter dependence on God and the reality of their great redemption, so that they might respond with lives of obedience and service. In the New Testament age it is much the same. All of life is described as worship (Rom. 12:1, 2), but the people of God are also called together to hear the word of God, to praise him and to pray together. Public and private worship motivates us to make God's name known among the people.

God-serving or Self-serving?

Often the Christian faith is seen as a fire escape from hell and not a call to service. Romans 8:29 has a different perspective: "For those God foreknew he also predestined to be conformed to the likeness of his Son, that he might be the firstborn among many brothers." The purpose of our redemption is to make us like Jesus Christ, the obedient Son who fulfilled all that God called Israel to be and to do. In the wilderness Israel failed to serve the Lord and actually served other gods, and many other times in history they failed in their calling as a servant nation. But Jesus Christ came to fulfill this servant calling. He served the needy people of Israel and his disciples. His servanthood climaxed during the Last Supper when he washed the disciples' feet: "Now that I, your Lord and Teacher, have washed your feet, you also should wash one another's feet. I have set you an example that you should do as I have done for you. I tell you the truth, no servant is greater than his master" (John 13:14-16). The Parable of the Good Samaritan is another model of this call to service (Luke 10:25-37). The service demonstrated there reaches out indiscriminately to one's neighbor, a neighbor being anyone whose need is known to us.

The definition of this service reaches back to creation where we are called to harness the creation for God (Gen. 1:26-28). *Ruling* and *subduing* mean serving God in his creation. No legitimate work falls outside of this category. There is no such thing as a "secular" task when it is performed by a redeemed person. Our motivation is the glory of God and our standards come from his law, which makes whatever we do a service for the King. So our concept of service must be holistic, including not just worship and witness but all of life's tasks.

In sharp contrast to Jesus' example and our own creation calling, much of our religious life today is self-serving. Many of us come to Jesus Christ out of deep personal need. We are right in seeing Jesus as the answer to those needs, but we must be careful not to turn the gospel upside down and behave as if we were meant to become Christians so that God could serve *us*. Too often our initial motivation of need makes our understanding of the gospel so emotional and subjective that it is nothing more than a self-centered life-style with a religious veneer. The popular books in the local Christian bookstore have such titles as *How to Be a Christian and Run a Successful Business* and *How to Manage Your Time*. Yet the story of the exodus starkly reminds us that we have been redeemed to serve. If we have not been saved from *selfishness* to *service* there is good reason to question whether we have been truly saved. Begin today to think of people whom you can serve. A concrete act of kindness to a person in need will often open the opportunity for a word of witness for Jesus Christ.

Our motive for service must be clear: we do not serve to be saved. But having been redeemed from the hand of the enemy, we serve the living God. "This is how God showed his love among us: He sent his one and only son into the world that we might live through him. . . . Dear friends, since God so loved us, we also ought to love one another" (1 John 4:9, 11). Having been so marvelously loved in Christ, therefore we love. The covenant mission of Christ is to bring restoration and reconciliation to a lost and needy world.

In Christ we are no longer slaves to sin but are free to serve Christ, motivated by thankfulness for our redemption and warmed and encouraged by our new status — sons who have the fullness of the Holy Spirit.

Note

1. Christopher Lasch, *The Culture of Narcissism* (New York: Warner Books, 1980), 147.

Review Questions

1. What is the full meaning of the Hebrew word for "worship"?

2. What is the difference between slavery and servant-hood? How does adoption help to explain the difference?

3. What is the difference between Israel's adoption and ours?

Discussion Questions

1. Respond to this statement: "Man is never truly free until he has freed himself from the chains of all religion, including Christianity."

2. What perspectives on our salvation come from a reflection on our adoption?

3. What people can you begin to serve today? Be specific: list individual needs that you plan to meet this week.

11

REMEMBER THIS DELIVERANCE!

The escape of some Hebrew slaves from Egypt could be considered a mere blip on the screen of history. The loss of some Egyptian soldiers and chariots would hardly be seen as a significant event. Historians today would probably record it as a mere footnote. But in the history of redemption, where God acts to fulfill his promises, the exodus stands out as God's most significant mighty act until the coming of the Lord Jesus Christ.

Our reflections on the Christian faith have often caused us to focus on its moral imperatives, its social implications, its theological order. But the central focus of the Christian faith must always be redemption. This chapter will show why this is so, and how the Old Testament writers have centered their thoughts on the exodus, the key redemptive act of the old covenant.

God liberates and saves Israel; therefore Israel's God is the God of salvation. Through this great moment of redemptive history God reveals himself. Through the exodus the people truly come to know God. This is not to say that Abraham and the patriarchs did not know him, but rather that from the exodus forward the people of God knew him more fully.

The Exodus and God's Sovereignty

God's redemptive actions reveal his sovereignty. The exodus redemption and God's name, *I AM WHO I AM*, reveal that God is what he is *because of his own nature*. He is not controlled by anything outside of himself. Nothing shifts the eternal purpose of God: from beginning to end God's plan of redemption expresses his self-determination and independence. It is not that he does not feel emotion, for he is moved by Israel's bondage. But what he does for Israel flows from his own nature as a person of love and justice. As a God of love he must deliver his people from their horrible slavery. But as the God of justice he must also judge Egypt — and even Israel — in the death and bloodletting of the Passover lamb. Redemption flows out of the character of a God of love and justice, not from the circumstances of the people. God's character constrains him to help Israel in their unworthiness and impotence. Israel was unworthy because they had worshiped the gods of Egypt and impotent in their slavery and oppression. Yet in his sovereignty God acts in faithfulness to his own nature and promise.

Well-meaning Christians often profess, "God can do everything." God *cannot* do everything, because he must be faithful to his own nature and attributes. The great truth powerfully revealed in Scripture is that God is faithful to his own nature.

The exodus teaches us two things about God:

Sovereignty underlies his actions toward Israel (Ex. 6:7);

In his love and justice he is faithful to himself and his word of promise (Ex. 3:15; 6:5-8).

The events of the New Testament show us these truths in all their fullness. God's word of promise is carried out and confirmed by his work of redemption. In our everyday experiences we get to know someone not only by what he says but also by what he does. If a person says something we watch to see whether his words are borne out by his actions. So it is with God. His redemptive work in Jesus Christ demonstrates to us his sovereignty (Eph. 1:4-8, Rom. 9:14-23), love (1 John 4:10, Rom. 5:8) and justice (Rom. 3:25, 26).

God expresses through his sovereignty both his love and justice; not one attribute at the expense of the other but both of them completely and concurrently at the cross.

Redemption must be constantly affirmed as the focus of our worship and obedience as Christians. Satan will constantly try to divert us from the simple reality of our redemption by the Lamb of God. It seems trite, but we must love the old, old story of Jesus' blood and sacrifice. The redeemed are taught to sing, "Worthy is the Lamb, who was slain, to receive power and wealth and wisdom and strength and honor and glory and praise! . . . To him who sits on the throne and to the Lamb be praise and honor and glory and power, for ever and ever!" (Rev. 5:12, 13). All our service, worship and obedience must echo the cry of the innumerable multitude, "Salvation belongs to our God, who sits on the throne, and to the Lamb" (Rev. 7:10).

The Exodus in the Old Testament

God's people have always been called to this perspective. We can clearly see this when we recall the pride of place given to the exodus in the Old Testament. At the time of Abraham, Israel's life as a nation was only a promise: "I will make you into a great nation" (Gen. 12:2). Israel's beginning lay in this crucial, historical event of the exodus. Before this time they had been either a nomadic clan or a group of slaves. So even the earlier events of the Old Testament demonstrate the centrality of the exodus. It is most likely that during the time of the exodus Moses gathered the existing documents and oral traditions and, under the inspiration of the Holy Spirit, recorded the book of Genesis and the early chapters of Exodus. While he did this he was conscious of what had already happened in the exodus, for through it God fulfilled his promise to Abraham and made Israel a nation.

Later Old Testament writers look back to three outstanding events in these early writings. They focus on Abraham, the exodus and the reign of David. Moses and the exodus event serve as the essential link between Abraham and David. The exodus made the promises to Abraham concrete, making way for a nation and a land over which David might rule. David conquered the land and provided, in his son Solomon, a temple where Yahweh would make his name dwell. But it is the exodus that provides all the potential for this ultimate Old Testament fulfillment. When even skeptical critics see the way the exodus dominates the message of the Old Testament and the life of Israel as a nation, they confess that such an event must have taken place. One such critic wrote, "A belief so ancient and so entrenched will admit of no explanation save that Israel actually escaped from Egypt to the accompaniment of events so stupendous that they were impressed forever on her memory."[1]

The Exodus and Old Testament Worship

At the center of Israel's life as a nation lay the moral law and the ceremonial worship. Obedience and worship are to be Israel's response to their deliverance, the fruits of their redemption. A nation thus redeemed by the blood of the lamb needs instruction and regulation. The Ten Commandments start with God proclaiming, "I am the LORD your God, who brought you out of Egypt, out of the land of slavery" (Ex. 20:2). Thus the entire Israelite ethic finds its purpose and motive in the exodus: "The alien living with you must be treated as one of your native-born. Love him as yourself, for you were aliens in Egypt. I am the LORD your God" (Lev. 19:34). The redemption of the exodus is often linked with Israel's ethical instructions, providing the reason and motive: "Do not use dishonest standards when measuring length, weight or quantity. . . . I am the LORD your God, who brought you out of Egypt" (Lev. 19:35, 36). Doesn't this command sound just like the ethical motive of the New Testament "for Christ has redeemed us"? Read and reflect on other texts that stress the same thing: Leviticus 18:3; 20:24ff; 26:13, 45.

Furthermore, when a person came to the temple to worship through the presentation of his firstfruits he was to confess, "My father was a wandering Aramean, and he went down into Egypt . . . . So the LORD brought us out of Egypt with a mighty hand and an outstretched arm, with great terror and with miraculous signs and wonders" (Deut. 26:5, 8). The exodus was intended to motivate gratitude and thus obedience. If God had done such great things for Israel, then they should dedicate themselves to keep his law. He kept his covenant; now Israel was to enter into that relationship and keep the covenant law, responding in thankful worship.

The word *remember* dominated Old Testament revelation. Used 107 times, it connected with the exodus to remind generation after generation that the nation owed its existence to the exodus. The word *remember* is often used to mean just the nostalgic recalling of an event, but the biblical writers used *remember* and *memory* in a very different way. *Remembering* meant "it is as if it happened to me." We have some experiences in American history that help us understand this use of *remember*. "Remember the Maine" was the rallying cry in the Spanish American War. That cry implied that every American was personally involved in what happened in Havana harbor. Furthermore, each person was called to action to avenge the affront. So *remember* meant personal involvement and commitment.

The ordinance that would remember the nation's rescue from Egypt would be the Passover celebration, including the Feast of Unleavened Bread. Israel reenacted the whole complex of events, from preparation for the flight and the haste with which they left to the passing over of the death angel (Ex. 13:11ff). So vivid was the drama that for some Jews the exodus "ceased to be a fact of the past and became a living reality."[2] We can imagine the children watching and in wide-eyed amazement asking, "What does it all mean?" Some of the Israelites made it plain to their children: "It is the Passover sacrifice to the LORD, who passed over the houses of the Israelites in Egypt and spared our homes when he struck down the Egyptians" (Ex. 12:26, 27; see also vss 28-30 and Deut. 16:1ff).

The people of God in every age must be ready to explain their ceremonies, especially to their covenant children. When believers' children ask the meaning of the Lord's Supper, believers must be prepared with answers that aren't formalistic but proclaim the heart of the gospel. The bread is the symbol of the body of Christ, for God's Son came to live a perfect life on our behalf. The wine symbolizes the blood of Christ because we deserve to die, but Christ died in our place. The sacrament "proclaims the Lord's death until he comes" and thus provides an opportunity to testify to the essence of the gospel.

Worship in the nation of Israel involved professions of faith or creedal ceremonies. Today we recite the Apostles' or the Nicene creed; in the Old Testament era they recited the great acts of God in the exodus. When the people brought the firstfruits and tithes to the temple the act began with a creedal profession: "Then you shall declare before the LORD your God: My father was a wandering Aramean, and he went down into Egypt" (Deut. 26:5). In the Christian era our confession of faith centers in the person and work of Christ; in the Old Testament period it centered in the exodus deliverance.

The Exodus in the Psalms

The book of Psalms gathers together much of the song and praise material of Israel. There are ten psalms with clear references to the exodus: 66, 77, 78, 80, 81, 105, 106, 114, 135, 136. Notice that when the psalmists sing praise to God as the Redeemer they take the exodus as their theme. A reading of a few psalms will illustrate this:

Psalm 66 declares a celebration of God's deliverance beginning at the exodus;

Psalm 114 is a vivid poetic description of God's great victory in the exodus;

Psalm 80 pleads with God to act now as he acted in the exodus, and Israel is described as both a flock and a vine.

The song material of God's people must always focus on praising God for his great redemption. While much of the hymnology of the church has been sentimental and personalistic, the psalms provide us with the great model for praise. We must praise God for his saving work. The songs must speak of the Lamb who shed his blood that we might live. They must praise the God who destroys our enemies so that the people of God might be saved. Are we singing some songs that fail to measure up to the model of praise for God's redemption? Are some of our modern Christian songs adequate in their praise to God for his justice — even his anger?

The Exodus in the Prophets

The exodus also has a dominant role in the Prophets. In the former prophets — in the books of Samuel and Kings — it is used as a starting point for their description of the nation and a basis for the prophets' call for repentance (see 1 Sam. 2:27; 8:8; 2 Sam. 7:6, 23; 1 Kings 6:1; 8:9, 16, 21, 51, 53). So too the latter prophets—e.g., Amos, Micah, Isaiah, Jeremiah — use the exodus as the basis for their call for repentance. Israel must see God's claim on them because of his redemption in the exodus and respond in repentance and obedience (see Amos 2:10; 3:1; Mic. 6:4; 7:15; Jer. 2:6; 7:22, 25).

These and many other passages make it clear that the saving work of God began when Israel was delivered from bondage in Egypt, albeit a nation that still needed to be saved from itself. And another important development takes place in the prophetic writings: Egypt is spiritualized. Egypt becomes the symbol of judgment that will come on Israel if they do not repent: "They offer sacrifices given to me and they eat meat, but the LORD is not pleased with them. Now he will remember their wickedness and punish their sins: They will return to Egypt" (Hos. 8:13; see also 9:3, 6).

The prophets develop the exodus even further into the idea of a "second exodus." The later enemies such as Assyria and Babylon will hold the people of God in bondage. The Assyrian general will seize Jerusalem (2 Kings 18:17ff, Is. 36:2ff). The Babylonians will carry them captive to Babylon. But God will deliver his people, acting in a way consistent with his actions in the exodus: " 'However, the days are coming,' declares the LORD, 'when men will no longer say, "As surely as the LORD lives, who brought the Israelites up out of Egypt," but they will say, "As surely as the LORD lives, who brought the Israelites up out of the land of the north and out of all the countries where he had banished them" '" (Jer. 16:14, 15). The climax of this exodus application is seen in the prophetic word given in the exile. Israel rebelled and turned to false gods, and therefore was taken into exile in Babylon; but "Then his people recalled the days of old, the days of Moses and his people—where is he who brought them through the sea, with the shepherd of his flock?" (Is. 63ff, Ezek. 20). All of these passages allude to a messianic figure who will deliver God's people. They were looking for the coming of the great Redeemer, Jesus Christ.

So all of the Old Testament writers—prophets, priests, historians, poets—look back to and build on the exodus. In various ways and with many nuances they say, "Yahweh is our God. Remember how he acted in the exodus? He is still the same today." The Old Testament Scriptures build their message on the exodus event; but more than that, they see it as the foundation for a new covenant. God will act in a way consistent with what he did in Egypt, but in a new and greater way. " 'The time is coming,' declares the LORD, 'when I will make a new covenant with the house of Israel and with the house of Judah. It will not be like the covenant I made with their forefathers when I took them by the hand to lead them out of Egypt . . . . This is the covenant I will make . . . . I will put my law in their minds and write it on their hearts. I will be their God and they will be my people' " (Jer. 31:31-33). The exodus events form the backdrop for all of God's saving work in the Old Testament, and they look forward to his great salvation in the New.

Notes

1. John Bright, *History of Israel*, 2nd ed. (Philadelphia: Westminster Press, 1972), 120.

2. Quoted in *The Exodus in the New Testament* (London: Tyndale Press, 1963), 8.

Review Questions

1. What is the focus of the Christian faith?

2. What two things does the exodus teach us about God?

3. How does the exodus link Abraham and David?

4. What did the Old Testament profession of faith center on? What does the New Testament profession of faith center on?

5. How do the prophets show the coming of Christ as a second exodus?

Discussion Questions

1. How do you explain the Lord's Supper to your children?

2. Study Psalms 66, 77, 80, 81, 105, 106, 114, 135 and 136. What elements of these psalms provide models for our worship?

3. How are God's subsequent acts in redemptive history consistent with the exodus? What does that tell you about God? How does that affect your view of the exodus?

12

CHRIST OUR PASSOVER AND OUR EXODUS

Throughout the Old Testament we find a restless onward movement that looks forward to the fulfillment of prophecy and promise in the Messiah. The history of Israel is dominated by promises, commands, threats, prophecies, typology — all of which find their ultimate fulfillment in Christ. Again and again the living God breaks into the lives of his people with his word of promise and command. As we have seen in our study, fulfillment of the promises made to Abraham often occur in the Old Testament itself. For example, by means of the exodus Israel became a nation prepared for possession of the promised land. The promised lines of prophets and priests began, someday to be completely fulfilled in Jesus Christ.

The Old Testament shows us that Jesus' ministry on earth harmonizes with God's dealing with his people throughout the ages (Luke 13:44). In Jesus Christ all the promises of God are *Yes* and *Amen* (2 Cor. 1:20, Rev. 3:14). He is the true object of all the signs, the true image of all the shadows. This does not mean that every promise was originally understood to be pointing to Jesus Christ, but these promises have an additional focus that is directed to the work that he came to do. So our knowledge of Christ and his work is incomplete without the Old Testament. The historical action of the Old Testament reminds us not only of his person but also of his work of redemption in history.

The exodus theology of the Old Testament can only leave men expectant; it cannot satisfy them. The Old Testament sets a pattern, an outline; the New Testament provides fulfillment. We will look at a brief outline of exodus material in the New Testament and then make some theological and practical applications. In the gospels we are confronted with one who claimed that his person, life and work were affirmed by the Old Testament. "This is what I told you while I was still with you: Everything must be fulfilled that is written about me in the Law of Moses, the Prophets and the Psalms" (Luke 24:44). This statement does not mean that we should see parallels to the Old Testament pattern in every detail of Christ's life. Every crossing of the Sea of Galilee could hardly be another exodus from Egypt. We need to be careful to maintain a biblical warrant for our conclusions.

But by the same token Christians have often failed to see the Christ-centered nature of the Old Testament. Whole books have been written on the exodus as a pattern for moving or directing large groups of people. Some have seen Moses as an example of obedience or disobedience, or as a pattern for church leadership. As we have noted, there is some truth to these observations; but the central message focuses on God's redemption of his people, ultimately fulfilled in Christ. This theme gives dynamic power and the reason for our life of obedience.

The Exodus in the Gospels

The pattern of the gospels as well as many allusions in them intend some theological reference to the exodus. John the Baptist's birth caused his father Zechariah to bless God in the overtones of the exodus (Ex. 3:16ff; 6:4ff). God had visited and redeemed his people. They had been saved from their enemies and had experienced mercy because God remembered his covenant. Also, the name *Jesus* given to the Lord at his birth comes from the Hebrew form of *Joshua*. The exodus was the first step of salvation that would climax when Joshua led God's people into the land. Further, Herod's attempts to kill Jesus, the second Moses, clearly recalls Pharaoh's attempt to kill the Hebrew children (Matt. 2:13-18, Ex. 1:16).

Even the taking of baby Jesus to Egypt relates to the background of the exodus. Matthew quotes from an Old Testament reference to the exodus: "Out of Egypt I called my son" (Hos. 11:1, Matt. 2:15). Jesus is both the source of the New Israel and the New Testament fulfillment of the firstborn son called out of Egypt (Ex. 4:22). There can be little question that Jesus' forty days in the wilderness were a miniature of Israel's forty years in the wilderness. Jesus began his earthly ministry by performing miracles. All of the gospel writers see these miracles as signs of the power of God at work, confirming divine authority and gaining victory over the oppressive forces of Satan. The controversy between Jesus and the teachers of the law over whether his power was from God or from Beelzebub seems to point to the power of the miraculous in the exodus. Jesus said, "But if I drive out demons by the finger of God, then the kingdom of God has come to you" (Luke 11:20). Recall how the phrase *finger of God* was used to describe the power of God in the plagues (Ex. 8:19).

In Matthew 5:21ff Christ speaks as the second Moses and his teaching both recalls and expands on the Pentateuch: "You have heard that it was said to the people long ago . . . . But I tell you . . . " Like Moses, the Prophet here gives the law from a mountain. Jesus does not speak of his disciples as the beginning of a New Israel; but the choosing of the twelve is a clear parallel to the twelve tribes of Israel (Matt. 19:28).

The transfiguration experience also was alive with exodus symbolism. Moses himself appeared with Elijah and Jesus. The Lord's face shone with the glory of God as did Moses' on Mount Sinai (Ex. 34:29). The appearance of the cloud and the voice of God from it were not something new in biblical revelation but clearly refer back to the pillar of cloud and the cloud on Sinai. The words "This is my Son, whom I love. Listen to him" (Mark 9:7) surely echo "The LORD your God will raise up for you a prophet like me . . . . You must listen to him" (Deut. 18:15). Clearest of all, however, is Luke's pointed reference to the reality that Jesus was talking to Moses and Elijah about *his* exodus (Luke 9:31). The mighty act of redemption effected in the exodus will have its ultimate fulfillment in Christ's death and resurrection. Through the transfiguration we see how God has woven a marvelous unity between the exodus and Christ's great redemption on the cross.

This episode also reminds us that our calling as God's people is to listen to Jesus Christ. Because of our sinful rebellion we listen to the spirits of our age and are driven in our values and attitudes by them rather than by Christ's word. But how are we to listen to Christ? In 2 Peter 1:16-21 the apostle tells us that in the Scriptures we have a prophetic word more certain and complete than his own experience on the mountain. Every believer would do well to spend more time reading, meditating upon and studying the Bible, and in living out Christ's commands.

Jesus' journey to Jerusalem focuses on the celebration of the Passover, that great exodus celebration. This celebration by Jesus was both the last Passover and the first Lord's Supper. Jesus' words, "This is my blood of the covenant, which is poured out for many" (Mark 14:24), echo what Moses said to Israel when the covenant was confirmed after the exodus: "This is the blood of the covenant that the LORD has made with you" (Ex. 24:8). The original Passover lamb and its blood are in view in Mark 14:24. The blood of the lamb had brought redemption and had made the covenant effective. The shedding of blood was prominent in the exodus Passover. It had been seen before in Abraham's cutting of the animals, and the practice was forcefully confirmed in the blood sprinkled on the doorpost and lintel. This wealth of Old Testament background enables us to see with clarity the reason for Christ's death and the shedding of his blood. Here we see pictured the truth that stands at the center of the Christian faith: Sin must be removed by the sacrifice of God's own Son. God's wrath brings the penalty of death; but the shed blood of the Lamb of God, Jesus Christ, takes away sin and delivers us from its consequence, death. Christians must never forget that we deserve death and ultimate judgment, but God in the person of his Son has borne that judgment for those trusting in him. The Christian faith has often been plagued by sentimental notions of the gospel — that Jesus saves us from ourselves or that he merely saves us from our sins. But we need to understand this dimension of God's impending judgment. To neglect that theme becomes unfaithfulness to God.

More than any other gospel writer, John invites his readers to think about Christ and his ministry in a metaphorical and symbolic way. In the first chapter of this gospel John the Baptist points to Jesus as the Lamb of God. Even earlier in the same chapter Jesus is presented as the one greater than Moses. John mentions Moses' vision of God: "For the law was given through Moses; grace and truth came through Jesus Christ. No one has ever seen God, but God the One and Only, who is at the Father's side, has made him known" (John 1:17, 18). Moses had several encounters with God, but Christ is *one with* God, and therefore climactically reveals God to his people. Surely John's readers would think of the Passover lamb when they read, "Not one of his bones will be broken" (John 19:36; see Ex. 12:46).

Moreover two Johannine titles of Christ have their origin in the exodus: Bridegroom of Israel (Jer. 2:2) and true Vine (Ps. 80:8). As Israel had the Lord as her bridegroom in the wilderness and she herself was the vine brought out of Egypt, so Christ is the bridegroom of his church and the true vine of which the church is the branch (John 3:29; 15:1). In John 6 the apostle links the Passover and the manna in the wilderness. A parallel is drawn between the death of God's only Son and the bread of the Last Supper. These events all occurred when "The Jewish Passover Feast was near" (John 6:4). Thus the parallel between Moses and Christ finds its focus in the exodus, the Passover, and the wilderness experience of the Old Testament. According to John, Jesus was declaring to his Jewish opponents the true significance of this festival. Indeed, the crucifixion took place at the time of the Passover. God's great plan of redemption is given shape and meaning in the Old Testament by the exodus, and in the New Testament the crucifixion is seen as the fulfillment of that great redemptive event.

In our Bible study it is important for us to see that the symbols and structure of the gospels are controlled by the Old Testament. We are not just New Testament Christians: as believers our roots go deeply into Old Testament soil. When we see the crucifixion and resurrection as the fulfillment of the exodus, the force of Christ's victory over his enemies — and our victory in him — become clear. Death is no more because the Passover lamb has been slain and Christ is alive: "He who believes in me will live, even though he dies" (John 11:25). In the everyday experience of our Christian lives we have access to a victory that calls us to obedience and faith. Paul says about Christ, "The death he died, he died to sin once for all; but the life he lives, he lives to God. In the same way, count yourselves dead to sin but alive to God in Christ Jesus" (Rom. 6:10, 11). We must act on the basis of a victory already won in the Lamb who was slain at Calvary.

The Exodus in Acts

There are many allusions to the exodus in the book of Acts, the clearest of which are found in Stephen's speech. A significant advance is about to take place. Until this time the message of the gospel is primarily directed to the Jews. But following the events of Acts 7 the church will be truly universal, inclusive of all races, nations and peoples. Just prior to this new step in the history of redemption, Stephen reviews Old Testament history and focuses on the exodus. He draws a clear parallel between Moses, the Old Testament redeemer rejected by God's people, and Jesus, rejected by Jews who perverted the meaning of Old Testament worship. Stephen calls them to leave the idolatry of that stiff-necked generation, come out of their rebellion and march on to the promised land of fullness in Jesus Christ.

The Exodus in Paul

Twice in Paul's letters we are confronted with exodus typology: "Christ, our Passover lamb, has been sacrificed. Therefore let us keep the Festival" (1 Cor. 5:7, 8). Believers have been redeemed by the blood of Christ and are called forth from their old way of living to a life of celebration and obedience. This text must be linked to the apostle's instructions concerning the Lord's Supper in 1 Corinthians 11:23ff. The words of Exodus 12:14, "This is a day you are to commemorate," emphasize that the Passover was a memorial. So too the Lord's Supper — "[D]o this in remembrance of me" (1 Cor. 12:24)—is a memorial to a new Passover lamb who brings deliverance to his people. Furthermore, in 1 Corinthians 10:1-10 Paul refers to the redemption at the Red Sea and the wilderness disobedience as "examples." Our baptism is like theirs, our spiritual food is like theirs. Our Savior — Christ, the Rock — is the same as theirs. Paul is saying that there is a spiritual sense in which we belong to that exodus generation, because the new exodus through the new Passover lamb, Jesus Christ, was simply a fulfillment of the Old Testament exodus.

We should see the Lord's Supper as one of the greatest privileges offered to Christians, yet often it becomes a merely formal act. The biblical connection of the Passover with the Lord's Supper reminds us of our responsibility not only to celebrate it but to do so with enthusiasm and gratitude. The sacrament of the Lord's Supper is a means provided by God for our growth in Christ and our dedication to him.

The historic tradition of many churches involves a pattern of preparation for the celebration of the Lord's Supper. The preparatory services would begin on Thursday evening and continue through Saturday, with sermons that called for self-examination and prepared hearts. A worship service on Monday morning concluded the season of preparation and observance with a call to go forth from the Lord's table with new zeal and dedication. How do *we* prepare for this solemn yet joyful feast? God's pilgrim church has been given this festival as a means of strength and growth until we arrive in the land of our heavenly rest.

The Exodus in Hebrews

The argument of the book of Hebrews rests on the dynamic newness and consequent superiority of the new covenant. Jewish Christians to whom this epistle was written were tempted to cling to tangible symbols of their Judaism. The author, like Stephen, uses the metaphor of their marching on to the spiritual promise of their full inheritance in Christ. Thus the epistle emphasizes that believers should not exchange the spiritual privileges of the new covenant for the merely outward, physical nature of the old. The metaphor of deliverance from Egypt and the inheritance of the promised land seems to be the organizing theme of the book.

Hebrews 3 compares the two "generations" of the people of God. Yahweh brought all of Israel out of Egypt, but only Caleb and Joshua entered the promised land. As believers today we are headed for the promised rest of our New Testament inheritance. Let us not, through disobedience, fail to enter! The rest symbolized in the promised land now becomes the fullness of our inheritance in Christ — heaven, the new heavens and the new earth.

Hebrews 6 and 10 warn about a judgment worse than the ones under Moses. God will judge those who are disobedient (Heb. 10:25ff, Deut. 32:35ff). But over against this terrible destruction there can be a better possession, the promised inheritance (Heb. 10:34, 36). If we are obedient we will soon be vindicated from the wrath to come. Like the heroes of Israel we must have a faith that produces obedience and looks to Jesus, the author and perfecter of our faith. We must seek a new city as a result of our new exodus in Christ and our subsequent pilgrimage as the people of God in the world. Christ, the great Shepherd who was brought up out of death as Moses was brought out of the Red Sea (Heb. 13:20f), has provided that redemption, the basis for our advance to the promised land of our full inheritance in Christ. That new relationship to Christ exists not for tomorrow or yesterday but for today. So God in effect warns, "Do not retreat to the formalism and immaturity of Judaism!"

The message of this epistle is still relevant. In our Christian lives we are often tempted to return to religious formalism or a salvation by works. The writer of Hebrews describes such a return as "immaturity." But we often turn to outward formalism or legalism because of Satan's temptation to doubt the sufficiency of Christ's redemption. In our lives, extra-biblical rules and a list of dos and don'ts seem so much easier than a spiritual wrestling with the clear principles of Scripture. We mustn't depend on a church or a man-made set of regulations but on Christ, who is the author and perfecter of our faith.

The Exodus in Revelation

Symbolism abounds in the book of Revelation and much of it comes from the exodus period. The imagery becomes clear when the lightning flashes, the thunder resounds and the trumpet calls (Rev. 4:5; 8:5, 6; see Ex. 19:16). Notice how the plagues of Revelation 8, 9 and 16 compare to the plagues against Egypt (Ex. 7-11).

Exodus	*Revelation*
Exodus 7:20 Blood	⟶ Revelation 16:3, 4
Exodus 7:25; 8:15 Frogs	⟶ Revelation 16:4
Exodus 9:9 Boils	⟶ Revelation 16:2, 21
Exodus 9:23 Hail	⟶ Revelation 8:7; 16:21
Exodus 10:1ff Locusts	⟶ Revelation 9:3ff
Exodus 10:21 Darkness	⟶ Revelation 16:10

This symbolism comes to a grand climax as the people of God join in singing the song of Moses and the Lamb, and we are given a vision of the sea of glass mingled with fire (Rev. 15).

We have seen how the exodus forms a basis for much of New Testament revelation by enabling us to see the person and work of Christ in their fullness. It especially enables us to see the glory and power of our redemption. Glorious words like *redemption, covenant, inheritance* and *rest* derive much of their meaning from the exodus. Moreover the exodus theme sounds a stern warning: Be sure you have entered into the redemption wrought by the Lamb. And in obedience press on to the promised land of your full inheritance in Christ.

> Today, if you hear his voice,
> do not harden your hearts (Heb. 3:7).

Review Questions

1. List some of the gospel allusions to the exodus.

2. What allusion to the exodus does Stephen make in Acts 7? How does he use the exodus to exhort his Jewish listeners?

3. How does Paul link Christians to the exodus?

4. What is the organizing theme of the letter to the Hebrews?

Discussion Questions

1. How does the transfiguration remind us to listen to Jesus Christ? How will you listen to Jesus Christ this week?

2. Is your observance of the sacraments merely a formal act? How can you make it a celebration? How can you turn the Lord's Supper into a feast?

3. Discuss the exodus theme in Hebrews. How does it bring out more vividly the warnings in that letter?

4. What new insights into the person and work of Christ did you learn from this chapter?

13

GOD AND EXODUS

There is nothing more boring than a theological essay that is unrelated to life. Our understanding of God and his purpose and nature must have an impact on real life. The book of Exodus relates theology to life with a series of dialogues between Moses and Israel and between Moses and God. As we have noted in our study, these events are recorded within a fascinating, dramatic and true story that begins with bullrushes and moves on to the Passover and the parting of the sea. God's revelation is not expressed in a philosophical or mystical form but in terms of real history, with human experiences in space and time. The result is a revelation and theology that relate powerfully to human experience. We are constrained to ask, What does it mean to be human beings under God?

Our final review of the exodus events should also recognize that there is hardly a single topic in the Old Testament or the New that is not contained in the exodus theme. Many of the themes used later in the Bible are first introduced here. It is appropriate that we conclude our study by considering a few salient points about the nature of God.

The God Who Controls

God controls all of history and all the circumstances of life. Nothing falls outside his power and control. He overruled Pharaoh's stubbornness to accomplish his purpose. The exodus was seen by the Hebrews as the supreme fact of history and an act of God on behalf of his people. The only possible explanation for this impossible event was that God had done it. This control by God has a purpose: he overrules all events for the ultimate good of his people and the glory of his name.

It is this great truth that gives hope to God's people. Secular forces may be oppressive and opposition to the gospel very powerful, but God is on his throne. The opening chapter of Exodus demonstrates that the very measures designed to repress the Israelites only made them multiply more (Ex. 1:12). There are a whole series of similar events that demonstrate the overruling, loving providence of God.

God Overrules

Preservation of Moses' life	Exodus 2:10
Fortunes of midwives	Exodus 1:21
Care for fugitive Moses	Exodus 2:15-22
Care for rebellious Israel	Exodus 16:3

What began as God's providential care over a nation and a man eventually proved to be an expression of God's grace. His control is always for the sake of his people and for the ultimate display of his favor and love, showered on the unworthy objects of his sovereign choice.

God Is Yahweh

God revealed himself to Moses as Yahweh, a name that was fundamental to the theology and ethics of the Mosaic period (Ex. 3:13-15). As we noted in Chapter 5, the word

LORD is usually used in our English Bibles to translate *Yahweh*. Exodus 6:3 seems to teach that, though the name was used previously in the book of Genesis, it has new depth and meaning in the context of the exodus experience. "I appeared to Abraham, to Isaac and to Jacob as God Almighty, but by my name *the LORD* I did not make myself known to them." In the Hebrew understanding, a name reveals one's character and attributes. To proclaim the name of Yahweh was to describe his character (Ex. 33:19). Since Israel belongs to Yahweh (Ex. 19:5) his name is involved in all that happens to them. So God cannot abandon Israel, because his reputation is bound up with them. He must get glory for his name through Israel, and in turn they are obligated to love and serve him.

Exodus 3:14 offers God's interpretation of the name: "I AM WHO I AM" or "I WILL BE WHAT I WILL BE." The text makes clear that the name is only explainable by God himself: only God can tell us who he is. The force of the verb to be is that Israel is not left to speculate about the existence or nature of God. Israel's God is there in history, active and revealing himself by word and deed. Furthermore the exodus itself defines the meaning of *Yahweh*. The creed of Israel will always define God as the one who brought them out of the land of Egypt. Yahweh is the God of salvation. The meaning of *I* AM WHO I AM or *I* WILL BE WHAT I WILL BE unfolds throughout history. More and more of God's nature is gradually shown. His name becomes richer.

Israel's and Our Profession of Yahweh

Exodus 20:2	Yahweh who led out of Egypt
Deuteronomy 26:9	Yahweh who led into Canaan
Judges 2:16	Yahweh who raised up judges
John 1:14	Yahweh the word in Christ

John 19:30   Yahweh's great work is finished
Romans 15:6   Yahweh the father of Jesus

So the name *Yahweh* means all that the name *Jesus* means. Each name lies at the heart of a new experience of deliverance and redemption. For the Hebrew, to say *Yahweh* reminded him of the exodus, just as to say *Jesus* for the Christian is to be reminded of the cross.

Often the Christian life turns inward to focus on our blessings and comforts. But all of these are the fruit of the covenant faithfulness of God. He will not abandon his people, because they bear his name. Our focus must be on the glory of his name and the redeeming power of his grace. Because God has saved us we are obligated to reflect his name in our lives. We see this principle in the Ten Commandments, which begin with Yahweh's saving act (Ex. 20:2) and continue with a call for the people of God to reflect his moral attributes. As Christians we bear the name of God. A name is not just a label: it means that Christlike attributes are to be seen in Christian people.

God Who Is Holy

God describes the place where he reveals himself to Moses as holy ground (Ex. 3:5). This is the first time that the word *holy* is used in the Pentateuch. *Holy* will become the predominant adjective used to describe God in Leviticus and the Prophets (e.g., Lev. 11:45). So Israel's relationship to God was not just intellectual, but moral. The knowledge of God involves more than acquiring facts about him: it includes a life of service and obedience. Demands are made of God's people because he is holy (Ex. 19:12, 13). "Be holy because I, the LORD your God, am holy"

(Lev. 19:2). Exodus 20-23 explains what it means to be the covenant people of a holy God.

We must never forget that, though our salvation is rooted in grace alone and received by faith alone, it will result in obedience and holiness.

> For it is by grace you have been saved, through faith . . . For we are God's workmanship, created in Christ Jesus to do good works (Eph. 2:8, 10).

God Who Remembers His Covenant

Yahweh "remembered his covenant" (Ex. 2:24). Can God forget? Only insofar as forgetting is a metaphor for forgiveness. To say that God remembers is an anthropomorphism (describing God with a human attribute to help us better to understand him.) Yahweh specifically remembers his covenant with Abraham, meaning that he remains true to his promises and purpose. Yahweh's plans cannot be arbitrary. Everything that has characterized his past relationships with humans will be valid for the present. In the exodus he remembered past promises and acted in history, so Israel would measure all subsequent history by the exodus. From this the people of God draw their assurance and hope. As they remember what God has done it will be a spur and encouragement to obedience (Ex. 2:20). Grace and law join together when God's people remember his salvation.

We have seen that the whole movement of salvation that culminated in the covenant at Sinai was the fulfillment of divine promises made to Abraham (Ex. 3:15-17). To the Hebrew mind, for God to remember is to act. God acts to keep his promise. To say that God remembers is to assert that he continues his saving grace to his people, fulfilling his promise and demonstrating self-consistency. For God's people to remember is also to act, out of gratitude and obedience in response to his grace.

We have also noted that Yahweh is the God of Abraham, Isaac and Jacob (Ex. 3:6). This truth asserts a lasting quality in the covenant relationship that God establishes with his people — even beyond the grave. From Christ himself comes this affirmation of the personal immortality of the patriarchs: "But about the resurrection of the dead—have you not read what God said to you, 'I am the God of Abraham, the God of Isaac, and the God of Jacob'? He is not the God of the dead but of the living" (Matt. 22:31, 32). God's covenant relationship with the patriarchs guarantees their continuing human existence. In New Testament terms it is a life that never passes away. In the simplest sense, inasmuch as God still remembers the patriarchs they must still exist. The hope for ultimate deliverance from death rests in God's remembering his covenant. So the psalmist reaches out in hope: "And I—in righteousness I will see your face; when I awake, I will be satisfied with seeing your likeness" (Ps. 17:15).

God Who Redeems and Saves

The words of Exodus 3:8 — "So I have come to rescue them from the hand of the Egyptians" — introduces the idea of salvation and redemption. These concepts were present earlier in Scripture (Gen. 8, 19), but the richness and fullness of both these words became clear in the deliverance from slavery (Ex. 3:10). God in his mercy and justice rescued the oppressed and helpless from the hand of the enemy. And it was not enough that he saved them from

Egypt: he fed and protected them and finally brought them into a rich inheritance—the land of Canaan.

In the context of our study, such future hope must be constantly translated into New Testament terms. The New Testament translates the promise of the land of Canaan into spiritual treasure, including the fullness of our inheritance in Christ (Heb. 11:14-16). There was one moment when the saving work of God came to its zenith in the exodus: namely, the crossing of the sea. Through that event Israel passed from death to new life (Ex. 14:30, 31). Pharaoh was the enemy who held in his hand the power of death (Ex. 5:2), and it was over him that the Lord triumphed. So the crossing of the sea was to Israel what the resurrection is to the Christian church. The power of darkness was defeated and God's people were saved (Ex. 14:30). The appeal in the New Testament to the faithfulness of God rests on the gift of his Son (Rom. 8:32); in the Old Testament it rested on the act of God in the exodus (Judg. 6:13).

Our study of the exodus constantly reminds us that redemption has to do with the political and social dimensions of life as well as individual reconciliation to God. Unfortunately evangelism usually means *personal* evangelism; but evangelism must speak to the impersonal structures of society. There must be a social action in our evangelical understanding of discipleship.

The church's ethical agenda has almost always been individualized, with concerns about alcohol, dancing, smoking, and so on. But the church must also challenge such evils as institutional racism and the redlining of districts where blacks are moving in. Redemption as a biblical concept draws its fundamental significance from the social and political deliverance from Egypt. The New Testament promises a new creation (2 Cor. 5:17). Salvation and redemption are related not only to individuals but to the world. The church must seek ways to bring change to individuals *and* systems—not simply charity but also justice. In the name of Jesus Christians must cry, "Because I love you, I do for you what is right."

God Who Acts in Substitution

The exodus brings before us not only the centrality of salvation and redemption but also the principle of substitution. God had said that death was the penalty for sin (Gen. 2:17). If the sinner is to live someone must take his place. So the Passover night marks the actual redemption of Israel (Ex. 12:29-32).

The death of the Passover lamb as the substitute for sinful Israel becomes central to the rich symbolism of the New Testament. Paul considered Christ's sacrifice to be the reality foreshadowed by the death of the Passover lamb. The Passover was not in the strictest sense a sacrifice, let alone a sin offering. This is evident from the sacrificial system detailed in the book of Leviticus. Rather, the Passover was associated with the shedding of blood and the notion of substitution. A victim had to die so that the firstborn of the house might live. The Passover also turned aside the wrath of God represented by the death angel. All of this prepares us for God's mightiest act of all — at the cross. The New Testament concludes that the actual work of salvation was accomplished there (Col. 2:14, 15).

God Who Judges

God also acts in anger even with his servants (Ex. 4:14). He maintains an unchanging attitude of judgment on sin —and on the sinner, unless he repents. The Old Testament does not speak often of attitudes such as anger and wrath but rather of the acts of God. The plagues and the overthrown chariots were signs of his anger. It is important to note that the parting of the sea brought judgment to the oppressor and salvation to the oppressed.

The cause of God's anger against his people was their unfaithfulness. God's wrath is never arbitrary. Stubborn opposition in his enemies (Ex. 14:4) and unfaithfulness in his servants (Ex. 32:7-10) arouse his anger.

Much of our modern preaching and teaching has left out this element of God's nature. When was the last time you heard a sermon on God's anger? The God of covenant mercy is also a God of covenant judgment. God's glory is the major issue of his work in the midst of his world; thus all his attributes manifest his glory, including his wrath (Ex. 24:17). Whether he acts in salvation or in judgment, all his acts glorify his name.

God Who Speaks

Throughout our study we have emphasized that the exodus demonstrates the pattern of promise and fulfillment: God reveals himself by word and deed. This truth is illustrated in Exodus 3:4-22. The appearance of God in the burning bush involved his word of revelation to Moses. So God's act together with his interpretation of it constitute revelation. As we have seen, the word often comes before the act; first comes the promise, then the fulfillment of that promise. An interpretation of the act is often included as well. "I am the LORD your God, who brought you out of Egypt." In fact, the call of Moses at the burning bush set the pattern for later prophetic calls (Ex. 3:1-6). At Yahweh's command the prophet spoke the word that Yahweh had first spoken to him (Ex. 16:23).

This pattern of act and interpretation has been written down in the Bible. The Bible does not consist of human insights into God's nature but is the story of how he chooses to reveal himself. This self-declaration by God finds its climax in the coming of Jesus Christ, God's word become flesh (John 1:1-5). God has fully acted and declared himself in his Son.

For the Christian, that revelation is found in the Bible. One of the most important elements of the Christian life is listening to God by reading the Scriptures. When we read and study the Bible with open hearts and minds God instructs, encourages, commands and tells us about himself. With the completion of the Bible we no longer meet God at a burning bush or at Mount Sinai, but each of us can meet him and hear him just as clearly and vividly whenever we open our Bibles.

Review Questions

1. List the attributes of God that are revealed in the exodus.

2. How does God's revelation follow an "act-interpretation" pattern? Cite some examples of this pattern in the Bible.

Discussion Questions

1. What comfort does the exodus provide to the Christian? What warnings does it offer for your life?

2. Do you agree that redemption is not strictly individual? How can your church broaden its "ethical agenda"?

3. Does your lifestyle reflect that of a slave or that of a servant? In what concrete ways can you demonstrate servanthood?

For Further Reading

The following books were influential in the writing of *Slavery to Servanthood*. Chapters where the work was most helpful are listed after each reference.

Cole, R. Alan. *Exodus: An Introduction and Commentary*. London: Tyndale Press, 1973.

Chapter 13

Kline, Meredith G. *By Oath Consigned: A Reinterpretation of the Covenant Signs of Circumcision and Baptism*. Grand Rapids: Eerdmans, 1968.

Chapter 2

Kline, Meredith G. *Images of the Spirit*. Grand Rapids: Baker, 1980.

Chapter 9

Nixon, R. E. *The Exodus in the New Testament*. London: Tyndale Press, 1963.

Chapters 11 and 12

Vos, Geerhardus. *Biblical Theology, Old and New Testaments*. Grand Rapids: Eerdmans, 1948.

Chapters 2 and 5